STEADFAST LOVE

For general information about other Minirth-Meier Clinic branch offices, counseling services, educational resources and hospital programs, call toll-free 1-800-545-1819. National Headquarters: (214)669-1733 (800)229-3000

STEADFAST LOVE

Dr. Frank and Mary Alice Minirth
Dr. Brian and Dr. Deborah Newman
Dr. Robert and Susan Hemfelt

A
JANET
THOMA
BOOK

THOMAS NELSON PUBLISHERS
NASHVILLE

Copyright © 1993 by Brian and Deborah Newman, Frank and Mary Alice Minirth, Robert and Susan Hemfelt

All rights reserved. Written permission must be secured from the publisher to use or reproduce any part of this book, except for brief quotations in critical reviews or articles.

Published in Nashville, Tennessee, by Thomas Nelson, Inc., and distributed in Canada by Lawson Falle, Ltd., Cambridge, Ontario.

Scripture quotations are from the NEW KING JAMES VERSION of the Bible. Copyright © 1979, 1980, 1982, Thomas Nelson, Inc., Publishers.

Library of Congress Cataloging-in-Publication Data
Steadfast love : the third passage of marriage / Brian Newman . . . [et al.].
p. cm.
ISBN 0-8407-4551-6
1. marriage—United States. 2. Interpersonal relations.
3. Communication in marriage—United States. I. Newman, Brian.
HQ734.S849 1993
306.81—dc20 92-23733
CIP

Printed in the United States of America
1 2 3 4 — 96 95 94 93

Contents

Acknowledgments

THE AUTHORS wish to thank the many people who helped make this book possible. Many thanks to Sandy Dengler and Catharine Walkinshaw, whose writing talents brought the illustrations, thoughts, and notes from the authors to a consistent and readable form. We also thank Janet Thoma for the many hours she spent guiding, editing, and directing the completion of the manuscript. We recognize Laurie Clark and Susan Salmon for their editorial assistance and attention to the details that helped make the book complete. Lastly, we acknowledge our children: Rachel, Renee, Carrie, and Alicia Minirth; Rachel and Benjamin Newman; Katy, Kristin, and Robert Gray Hemfelt, for the special part they add to our passages through marriage.

Chapter 1

The Passages: Growth Stages of a Living Marriage

*I*t was the best of times, it was the worst of times. Well, come to think of it, there wasn't much "best" about it. Rick and Nancy had reached an impasse in their marriage that made just about every day far from best. They were both working, but they couldn't get ahead of the bills. Their financial trouble was nothing serious, nothing to scream "bankruptcy!" about. They were just a little short all the time.

Rick was boring in his predictability. So was sex. Was Nancy that predictable too? She hated to think so. Naaah, surely not. Nancy didn't feel a day over twenty; she was still young, despite the somewhat expanded waistline and the fine little lines in the corners of her eyes.

Nancy's mother-in-law, Ethyl, was a royal pain and getting worse. The nosy woman thought Rick and Nancy ought to be buying a house by now instead of renting. Ethyl even offered to loan them some funds for the down payment. She thought they were too hard on their girls—or too lenient. Ethyl would play it both ways. And she was constantly complaining that Rick didn't pay enough attention to her. After all, she and Rick's father were not as spry as they used to be, and they ought to be seeing their grandchildren more regularly, and . . . The old woman. She never seemed to let up. And Rick's dad was difficult in the opposite direction. All he did when they visited was watch TV in the other room.

When a disagreement came up between Nancy and Rick—and that happened a lot—Nancy was having more and more trouble bringing the girls over to her side. They seemed to be siding with their father more frequently. Why couldn't they see when he was wrong?

Hints of Trouble

Nancy's glum mood is somewhat like the weeds in her garden. When she put in the flower bed out front, she had to disenfranchise a lot of dandelions and hawkweed. She pulled them, and her flower bed looked pretty good for awhile. But the dandelions and hawkweed kept coming back. So did the sorrel. Pull up a sorrel and you have stringy roots three feet long running to all the other sorrel weeds.

The problem in Nancy's flower bed and in her marriage was that she was not getting rid of the taproots: the part of the weed that sprouts more and more roots. So long as a bit of dandelion root remains—and it's next to impossible to pull a dandelion and get the whole taproot—the weed keeps returning. Unless you dig out all those strings, sorrel is yours forever.

When couples enter our counsel, we begin by listening to surface complaints, the parts of the weeds that show. Rick and Nancy's frictions above would fall into that category. Then we search for the underlying reasons for the friction. Until the hidden problems are rooted out and handled, we cannot resolve the surface symptoms permanently. Then the same roots will keep showing up, over and over.

How is your own marriage doing? Have you been picking up any hints of trouble? Do any of the following sound familiar?

_____ Chronic financial discomfort or distress?

_____ In-law problems or difficulties? Are they overinvolved?

_____ Family imbalance, such as us-versus-them? Family stress? Friction? Discipline problems?

_____ Any emotional or psychological dysfunctions in family members? Addictions, compulsions, or the like? Persistent habits the members can't seem to shake?

_____ Boredom or problems in the bedroom? Reduced frequency of romantic encounters? No outside love interests, are there?

_____ Any signs of aging in you and your spouse that really disturb you?

Nancy and Rick could check at least five of these. They had some things to work out. So might you.

One of the biggest taproots that continually causes surface problems is a failure of the marriage to move into the next passage when it ought to.

The Passages

Out of the forest, in a cloud of dust, with the thunder of running shoes, it's a . . . a . . . an orienteer? You're kidding. Here's this joker with a map in one hand and a compass in the other. He is in running shorts and a T-shirt, his legs all cut and scratched from underbrush, his brow sweaty. Mud cakes his running shoes.

Glowing with elation, he darts across the finish line and hands his card to the judges. The judges will confirm that he successfully checked in at each control point. He hasn't won yet; others are still on the course, and top prize goes to the fastest finisher who has completed all the checkpoints; but he has finished. Had he missed a checkpoint he would have been disqualified.

You don't dare follow other runners; they may have a different map and course. And you can't just trot through the course with your eyes on your compass. You must align your compass so many degrees and locate a reference landmark, make your way via the landmark to a flag-marked point, then align your route so many degrees to the next landmark and thereby, eventually, to the next checkpoint. Over hill and dale, fence and creek, road and woodlot, they run.

Actually, it's a lot of fun. A good orienteer can think clearly even when he or she is physically exhausted. For beginners, the challenge is not being the fastest, but just finding every checkpoint on their map. The experienced know the balance between running fast and using the best of their knowledge to find each checkpoint quickly and efficiently.

An orienteer is a master of intertwining tasks, if you will. The best time may not be achieved by running directly from point to point. The seasoned orienteer knows the great value of using a map to his/her advantage—taking a shortcut when it saves time, going around a mountain instead of straight over the top to save valuable physical energy. It's a rowdy, pell-mell sport with a soupçon of danger, requiring great skill and knowledge.

Exactly like marriage.

The runner has fun. In a good marriage, so do the spouses. Marriage takes skill and knowledge. Muddling through doesn't finish the race, and the whole point of marriage, as with a race, is to cross the finish line, having completed the full course. You're going to get scuffed up along the way. That comes with the game. You must clear each checkpoint in turn or you'll find yourself hopelessly off course and out of the race.

The checkpoints of a marriage we call passages. As the marriage moves from one of these passages to another—from checkpoint to checkpoint in an orienteering race—the marriage also moves through specific conditions common to the human race. Crisis and conflict, intimacy, forgiveness, children, and memories form some of them.

Every marriage moves through these passages at about the same rate. Divorced persons in a remarriage may truncate a passage, or prolong it a little, but the passages remain a constant.

Not counting pre-marriage, which is a phase in itself, we have divided marriage into five distinct passages. They are:

- The First Passage—New Love: the first two years / Whether the couple be eighteen years old or eighty, they pass first through this dewy-eyed stage of idealized love. Persons who have been married previously may go through it a little faster than those married for the first time, but everyone tastes its heady joy.
- The Second Passage—Realistic Love: from the second anniversary through the tenth / Kids and career put the push on. About now, too, a heavy dose of reality sets in. This perfect partner is not so perfect after all. If this is Eden, then why the thorns?
- The Third Passage—Steadfast Love: from the tenth anniversary through the twenty-fifth / Wrapped up in career, kids,

and a host of extraneous, time-consuming activities, the couple find themselves fallen into a rut. Either they're moving along complacently or they are at each other's throats, but there's a predictability about the whole relationship. Change is necessary and desirable.

- The Fourth Passage—Renewing Love: from the twenty-fifth through the thirty-fifth anniversary / As the kids fledge and careers peak, the meaning and purpose of life alters forever. Now what?

- The Fifth Passage—Transcendent Love: beyond the thirty-fifth anniversary / What a history this couple has! The texture of the marriage changes as the couple enter retirement, watch youth fade forever, and search for the ultimate meanings of life and death.

At the starting line, upon the word *go* orienteers can open their map, viewing it for the first time, and begin their race. Landmarks noted on each map serve as clues to the location of each checkpoint. (Orienteers are good at reading topographic maps, but they're equally good at reading weird little squiggles and cryptic abbreviations.) In a marriage, too, the couple starting out haven't a clue as to what really lies ahead, no matter how much pre-marital material they absorb. Only when you get out on the course does the map mean anything.

The landmarks used to negotiate each marriage passage (checkpoint) are called tasks. And the map to our race is shown on page 21. Unlike a race, though, you can work on more than one landmark/task at once. You use the tasks to complete the passage, as the orienteer uses landmarks to find a checkpoint.

Each of the passages must be appropriately dealt with if the next one is to count. You cannot miss or disregard a checkpoint and still find the finish line. Too, an orienteer is out of the race if he or she doesn't check in at each specified checkpoint.

Likewise, the tasks that accompany a passage of marriage must be completed before the next passage begins. By tasks we mean attitude changes one must make, relationship boundaries that must be set, emotional experiences that must be encountered, and jobs one must complete in order to maintain an intimate marital relationship.

Failure to complete the course disqualifies the orienteer. Failure to complete tasks of the various passages of marriage leaves the marital partners without a clear picture of their future together—they no longer know how to reach the finish line—and that all too often ends the marriage.

The Dynamics of the Passages

When Doctors Newmans or Minirth or Hemfelt deal with the marital problems of couples in their counsel, they deal with three entities: the husband, the wife, and the marriage itself, as if the marriage were a living, breathing organism. For it is. If a marriage is not growing, it is dying. When a marriage gets hung up in a passage, it ceases growing. Growth is essential, therefore.

By definition, then, *passages are predictable and necessary stages, involving the physical, the emotional, and the spiritual.* Through them, partners journey toward the lifetime goal of growth as individuals and as a couple.

"Yes," you protest, "but my marriage is different; nobody has a union like ours."

Don't be so sure. No matter how wacky, off-the-wall, mundane, travel-fraught or otherwise unusual your marriage is, it shares one thing in common with all other marriages: the passages themselves.

How Are We Doing So Far?

Assuming you've been married longer than ten years, how have you fared in the first two passages? Are you truly ready for the third?

Consider these questions. Would your answer be a simple "No, doesn't apply" or a "Yes, that's us," whether conditional or not?

_____ I feel I must win when disagreement crops up. I am convinced I am right most or all of the time.

_____ My spouse has this same driving, competitive need to win.

_____ Forgive my spouse? You gotta be kidding. No. Not yet, at least.

_____ My spouse *still* doesn't really know what turns me on and satisfies me sexually.

_____ But then, we've never discussed sexual matters and techniques.

_____ I suspect or know of significant sexual problems or inhibitions that my parents had/have had.

_____ Likewise, my spouse's parents have had sexual difficulties they never resolved.

_____ Looking over that display page listing passages and tasks, I can say that my parents have not really completed their passages satisfactorily to date.

_____ Neither have my in-laws.

_____ My spouse's bad points outweigh the good ones.

_____ The kids are a major source of friction.

_____ Our marriage won't stabilize until the last kid moves out.

_____ I'm afraid our marriage will fall apart after the last kid moves out.

_____ This marriage is nothing like what I thought or hoped it would be.

_____ Frankly, I think I'm missing out, and I'm disappointed.

A "yes" answer to more than half of these questions, even if you had to qualify it to fit your circumstance, is cause for concern. Now ponder the following statements. Check those that apply to your situation.

1. _____ "Having shared a number of years of marriage together, I can honestly look at my spouse and say, 'You're someone special. I like you. I still find a fascination with the mystery of who you are. I'm still in love with you.' "

2. _____ "I can think of three specific features, characteristics, or attributes of my spouse that I still cherish now." *(For example, or add your own:*
   • *"You have a clever and spontaneous sense of humor that always keeps our relationship fresh."*
   • *"You have deep spiritual values, which have helped sustain us in the most difficult times."*

- *"You have a sexy body; after this many years of marriage, I still catch myself watching you walk across the room."*)

_____

_____

_____

3. _____ "I have seen you in the illusion of courtship. I have seen you in the difficult moments of stark reality. I have come to appreciate the whole of you in mature love, as much or more as in early love. Specifically, I appreciate the following strengths you have demonstrated in our most challenging crisis:" (For example, "In times of great stress, you become more outspoken in your loyalty to me rather than blaming me for the problem.")

_____

_____

_____

4. _____ "I appreciate the boundaries we have established with our children. We have reached that special balance between union and separateness in both our individual and couple relationships with each child."

5. _____ "No child in our family feels excluded or favored, and no child has been moved into the position of ally or surrogate with one parent against (or in place of) the other parent."

6. _____ "If children have not entered or remained in this marriage, due to choice, infertility, miscarriage, or premature death, we have both grieved this void."

Here's where a "yes" answer is good. If you can answer most of these statements in the affirmative, you successfully navigated the course through checkpoints one and two. You are on your way to three.

On the other hand, if most of your answers in the above section were not affirmative, your marriage may have gotten off course. You might want to recheck the map by reviewing those tasks necessary to complete the First and Second Passages of marriage. You'll find them in our first two books: *New Love*

(Nashville: Thomas Nelson, 1993) and *Realistic Love* (Nashville: Thomas Nelson, 1993) in this series on the passages of marriage.

This series, of which this book is number three, is based on relevant portions of the large hardcover edition of *The Passages of Marriage* (Nashville: Thomas Nelson, 1991) by the Minirths, the Hemfelts, and the Newmans. In addition, each book in this series contains new and expanded material not found in that original best-seller.

We invite readers at any passage of marriage to read all five of the books in this series. Since, however, some readers may be interested in only the book pertaining to their immediate passage, we have found it necessary to repeat certain themes from book to book.

What Marks the Third Passage?

We almost called this book "Complacent Love." *Complacent* is such a miserable word, but it defines many third-passage marriages. The terms *holding pattern, predictable,* and *disenchanted* also come to mind.

All of these terms are negative, and third-passage marriages, even those that could use a little help, need be nothing like those terms. With this book we hope to dispel the negatives in your union and replace them with positives. A side benefit of improving and invigorating your marriage at this stage is that your children will benefit.

(If you encounter serious emotional reactions as you explore your third-passage marriage, we urge you to consider seeking competent psychiatric, psychological, or marriage and family therapy professionals. Reading a book is never a substitute for professional therapy when therapy is necessary.)

"Yes, but my kids are teens, or nearly so!" you insist.

"And teens benefit immensely when their family unit is improved," we assure you.

Your family is going to be buffeted by losses in these next few years, and by frictions and forces that were latent until now. Exploring passage three can help you become aware of these frictions and forces and we will teach you to combat them. Deeper understanding of this passage can help you help yourself to become a happier, more contented person within your marriage. And we can help you and your spouse prepare for the future of your marriage.

The Future Is Now

Rick and Nancy, visiting their best friends, the Walkers next door, had just finished a rousing game of Pictionary™. Nancy and Barb, pitted against Rick and Larry, had won handily. Now Nancy, the pad of paper and pencil still before her, played a little game of her own.

Barb came out of the kitchen with the coffeepot. Nancy wrote *Just half a cup* on her pad.

"Coffee?" Barb asked Rick.

"Just half a cup," Rick replied.

As Larry started to put the game away, Nancy wrote "*I don't know yet.*"

Larry asked Rick, "Want a ride downtown tomorrow?"

"I don't know yet." Rick sipped at his coffee. "Good coffee, Barb. French roast?"

Good coffee was already on her pad. Nancy would not have anticipated the *French roast,* but she knew it was the only coffee variety Rick knew. She could have guessed.

She tossed the pad across the table to Larry. He glanced at it, looked at her curiously, and tucked the pad into the box.

Every word. She could just about predict every word from Rick's mouth! She thought like he did, waited on him, waited for him, crabbed at him, got crabbed at. They were mushing together into one big, unwholesome glob. She wasn't Nancy anymore, she was a plain, dumpy old Missus.

She hated it.

She hated herself, she hated Rick, she hated this whole ugly thing that marriage becomes after fifteen-plus years. No, maybe she didn't hate. *Hate* is a violent emotion, a vivid feeling. She didn't feel vivid. She felt blah. Her identity and her marriage's identity were lost—absorbed into "The Blob." How did it happen and what could Nancy do about it?

Let's deal first with the foremost of the Third Passage's tasks: Rebuilding a personal identity, for the sake of a healthy marriage and a healthy you.

Major Tasks of All the Passages of Marriage

THE FIRST PASSAGE–NEW LOVE
(The First Two Years of Marriage)

Task 1: Mold into One Family
Task 2: Overcome the Tendency to Jockey for Control
Task 3: Build a Sexual Union
Task 4: Make Responsible Choices
Task 5: Deal with Your Parents' Incomplete Passages

THE SECOND PASSAGE–REALISTIC LOVE
(From the Second through the Tenth Anniversary of Marriage)

Task 1: Hang On to Love After Reality Strikes
Task 2: Childproof Your Marriage
Task 3: Recognize the Hidden Contracts in Your Marriage
Task 4: Write a New Marriage Contract

THE THIRD PASSAGE–STEADFAST LOVE
(From the Tenth Anniversary through the Twenty-fifth)

Task 1: Maintain an Individual Identity along with the Marriage Identity
Task 2: Say the Final Good-byes
Task 3: Overcome the Now-or-Never Syndrome
Task 4: Practice True Forgiveness
Task 5: Accept the Inevitable Losses
Task 6: Help Your Adolescent Become an Individual
Task 7: Maintain an Intimate Relationship

THE FOURTH PASSAGE–RENEWING LOVE
(From the Twenty-fifth Anniversary through the Thirty-fifth)

Task 1: Combat the Crisis of This Passage
Task 2: Reestablish Intimacy
Task 3: Grieve the Particular Losses of This Passage

THE FIFTH PASSAGE–TRANSCENDENT LOVE
(Beyond the Thirty-fifth Anniversary)

Task 1: Prepare for Retirement
Task 2: Continue Renewing Love
Task 3: Achieve a Transcendent Perspective
Task 4: Accept My One and Only God-given Life

Chapter 2

Can You Maintain Individual Identity Within Your Marriage?

"**'A**nd they all lived happily ever after.' Now go to bed." James Jorgensen closed the book and tapped five-year-old Jamie on the head. He looked at eight-year-old Lynnette on his other side. "You too."

Jamie wiggled down off the sofa. "Is Mommy coming home tonight?"

"I don't know. She'll come wake you up and say goodnight, if she does. Brush your teeth."

"Don't forget to kiss me and tickle my nose. You forgot that last night."

"I'll try."

Jamie hustled away upstairs.

Lynnette sat, still staring at the book. "Is Joci gonna die?"

"Modern medicine performs all kinds of miracles. I sure hope they can help her. Let's pray hard that the Lord's will be done and that He'll be merciful."

"She's only two."

What could he say? James said nothing.

Lynnette slid to the edge of the sofa and stood up. "They don't really live happily ever after, do they?" She slogged upstairs like an old woman.

James watched her go. The worst thing about little Joci Jorgensen's cancer was not all the time his wife, Lonna, spent at the hospital with her. It wasn't the pain of being unable to help your helpless little girl. It certainly wasn't the financial burden of trying to cover what insurance did not. The worst thing was the way it robbed an eight-year-old of her innocence.

James received the call at ten. He asked Lonna's mother to stay with the children and joined his wife at the hospital for their last sorrowful vigil. It ended at three A.M.

The doctor looked nearly as haggard as Lonna did. "There was nothing we could do," he said. "We tried, but the bone marrow transplant didn't take."

My Spouse Is Like an Old Shoe . . .

Five years ago. Joci died five years ago today. By closing his eyes, James could see every picture of the tiny girl in their old photo album. There weren't that many. The third baby is photographed a small fraction as much as the first two children.

He sipped his breakfast coffee. "I wonder what she'd be like today."

Across the table, Lonna glanced at him. "Happy. She had such a charming personality. I think she would have kept it."

James smiled sadly. Curious, the way he and Lonna did that. Their thoughts seemed so often on the same wavelength. He didn't have to mention that he was thinking about Joci. The anniversary date, a glance—that was enough.

. . . Comfortable, But Wearing Out

On the fifth anniversary of their daughter's death, James and Lonna demonstrated the best and the worst of the Third Passage. They knew each other so well they didn't have to explain their thoughts to each other. In fact, James and Lonna both did that a lot, as if they could read each other's minds. Too, they shared the trauma, literally, that sometimes comes with raising children. Five years did not obliterate the loss of their two-year-old.

However, as couples build a history together, they may become so melded that their individuality suffers. They may become codependent—that is, so unwholesomely enmeshed that they begin to lose personal identity. In the beginning, a couple's task is to forge a marital identity out of two diverse personalities. By this stage, the task is nearly the reverse: to maintain an individual identity along with the marriage identity.

The First Task: To Maintain an Individual Identity Along with the Marriage Identity

Many couples feel as Louis Ajanian did when he told us, "My first wife was like an old piece of clothing. And I was the same for her. You don't have any reason to throw it away, but you're getting kind of tired of it. It's become a part of you, and you identify with it and you love it. Still, you start feeling ho-hum, and maybe even a little bitter about it."

Louis remarried after his first wife's death. He was back in the passages of marriage with a brand new spouse and loving every minute of it. Even though he and Marj, his new wife, had both been married before and both felt they brought experience that would help them keep their balance in their new union, they still had to watch out for codependent tendencies in their new relationship together.

Codependency

Codependency is an irrational, slavish, and ultimately damaging dependence and mutual dependence between two persons. It is the failure to maintain appropriate individual identity in a romantic union.

The term arose years ago as Alcoholics Anonymous began its amazing work. Professionals began to understand that everyone in alcoholic families was profoundly touched by the chemical addiction, not just the drunken member of the family. Persons dependent upon alcohol or other drugs would do well with recovery, returning to near normalcy. But their families would fall apart. Just as the alcoholics were dependent on a chemical, so were their families codependent upon unhealthy relationship patterns they had learned in coping with the addiction.

The concept of codependency today has expanded far beyond that original definition involving chemical dependency. It now means that, whatever the reason, two people have become so completely tangled into each other that their personal identities are damaged or reduced. Each spouse's identity derives from the partner, not from the self.

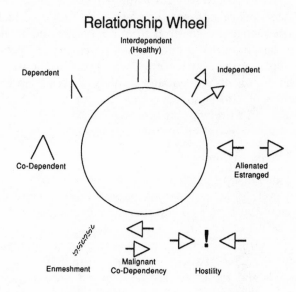

Relationship Wheel

The Codependency Wheel

Unexpected things happen to a marriage when codependency comes into play. Picture the spectrum of possibilities as a wheel, as in the accompanying figure. At the top lies wholesome interdependence. Interdependent couples have a rock solid commitment to remain together (parallel), but retain a healthy, friendly space between them, which allows for flexibility, creativity, and individuality. Should the couple drift down the wheel counterclockwise, one starts to lean excessively upon the other. They become progressively dependent upon each other. As they proceed down the wheel toward the bottom, it may appear that one leans more than the other, but in reality, deep down, both lean together.

At the bottom, malignantly codependent, these two have become so enmeshed that their individual identities are hard to sort out. Not even they themselves can do it. Instead, their lives seem to say, "I exist only as an extension of you." Sameness and dull complacency, interspersed with intense fighting—a desperate effort to avoid complete suffocation—result.

Conversely, if you travel down the wheel clockwise, exaggerated independence becomes damaging. At three o'clock, the couple has alienated themselves from each other and at the bottom, hostility has broken out—another form of codependency. Many couples at the bottom of the wheel oscillate between periods of enmeshment and agitated hostility. There is no balance. The malignant codependency says, "I can't live with him (or her). But I can't live without him (or her)."

How do people end up on this wild wheel?

False vs. Real Intimacy

Codependency problems can emerge anywhere in a person's life. However, for several reasons, persons in their Third Passage are extremely vulnerable. They are especially likely to slide down one side or the other of the codependency wheel. The codependent traits were probably present in the First and Second Passages, but this Third Passage exaggerates the traits.

The kids and the career are chugging along—no need any longer to go through the trials of getting either of them started. Assuming the couple either worked through such issues as control or else found a temporary truce, this Third Passage with its comfort, even complacency, offers special opportunity for greatly intensified intimacy. This is both a blessing and curse.

Deeper intimacy can be wonderful. But if old unresolved issues are still buried, this potential for intensified genuine intimacy becomes frightening. You might say increased intimacy threatens to open up the heart and let all the buried pain out to spread its poison. The insecure marriage partner unconsciously fears, "If this person gets to know me too well, he or she won't like me anymore."

Codependency is closeness of a sort, but it is false intimacy. Sliding down the wheel in either direction becomes a flight from genuine intimacy. By avoiding the real thing and substituting the false intimacy of codependency (which, for the person who grew up in a codependent family, is more comfortable anyway), that person need not risk being hurt; the pain can stay buried, unnoticed, festering.

The opposite of codependency is *not* (and this cannot be said too much) independence. The people traveling clockwise on the wheel are fiercely independent and getting more so all the time, headed for disaster. The opposite of codependency is interdependence. At the heart of interdependence lies genuine intimacy.

Genuine intimacy is a balance between enmeshment and friction, between dependence and independence. "Yes," says the well-balanced marriage partner, "I am dependent enough in my marriage to take down my mask and make myself vulnerable to you. I can openly share both my fears and joys. I am also independent enough to function as a complete person; I see us as two separate, autonomous people with divergent feelings."

Dr. Robert Hemfelt puts it this way, "Real intimacy requires the constant maintenance of this delicate balance. Fear prevents intimacy."

What Are You Afraid Of?

Frequently, Dr. Hemfelt asks the question of his clients: "What are you afraid of?" He catches people off guard. It's not a question they expect. And yet, its answer reveals much.

As two partners move down the wheel clockwise (the independent side), their lives diverge more and more. As they become ever more independent they disavow fear and need. "I don't need anyone or anything. I can make it on my own." Beneath that veneer of defiance, Robert Hemfelt finds a lot of fear and need.

What kind of fear? "Either that my intimacy needs won't be met," he responds, "or the fear of intimacy itself."

Couples *really* express surprise at the question when they are sliding down the counterclockwise (enmeshment) side. After all, they're pushing for sameness and identity with that other person. If that's not intimacy, what is? Actually, they're displaying the same fear of true, vulnerable intimacy as the persons who so wildly defend their independence. They aren't one individual person loving another different individual. Rather they have little identity of their own. An effort to become absorbed into another person, to dominate or be dominated, is not true intimacy. There is no unconditional love in that situation.

What About You?

So now we ask you: what are you afraid of? Down deep, what do you fear? We're not asking for your superficial phobias, although those can be crippling in their own right. Check any of the following if they apply. Or, add one of your own at the end.

_____ I'm afraid of being a failure as a wife/husband and/or mother/father.

_____ I'm afraid I'm not worthy of my spouse's love.

_____ I'm afraid of failing at my career.

_____ I'm afraid to let my true self be known to my spouse because she/he wouldn't like me very much if I did.

_____ I'm afraid to let myself be vulnerable, so I won't open up my innermost feelings to anyone. (You may feel this way because you were hurt sometime in the past when you opened up to someone).

_____ I'm afraid I'm not worthy of God's love.

_____ I'm afraid of abandonment. It is hard for me to trust that you love me and will choose to remain with me for a lifetime.

_____ I'm afraid that unless I'm controlling you or manipulating you, you will drift.

_____ I'm afraid to be assertive. I fear that any effort to stand up for myself will trigger your rejection of me.

_____ _____

_____ _____

You may find it difficult to list your innermost fears. But you must identify your fears before you can overcome them. This becomes one of the first steps in healing the codependency patterns.

How Does Codependency Begin?

How does one combat this fear and keep from sliding down either side of the codependency wheel? Dr. Hemfelt discussed the onset of codependency and how to combat it with a radio talk show host recently. "Most frequently," Dr. Hemfelt began, "the present is shaped by the past. Unless I can look beyond surface enmeshment or conflict in marriage, I'll end up shadow-boxing for the rest of the marriage. I'll be combatting surface symptoms—swatting at the shadows—without getting at the root: the problem casting the shadow. You can't deal with something until you know what you're dealing with. And for most of us, the roots of our codependency go back to the family we grew up in. In essence, if I have never said hello to the pain from my family–of–origin, I can't say good-bye to it."

Host: "What family-of-origin pain?"

Dr. Hemfelt: "Some sort of breakdown in the family you grew up in. To keep it simple, think of two categories of sources for problems: active abuses and passive abuses."

Host: "Active abuse, sexual abuse, physical violence, that kind of thing?"

Dr. Hemfelt: "That's right. Emotional or verbal violence. Parents inflicting their own needs or pain onto their children. And authority abuse, the parent never gave the child sufficient autonomy as he or she matured. Kids need increasing responsibility and freedom as they mature.

"And there's spiritual abuse, where the parent acts as a god in the child's life."

Host: "Isn't that often the way it is?"

Dr. Hemfelt: "Yes, especially at first. It's appropriate when kids are very small. But in later childhood and teens, healthy kids should be finding God individually. If the parents are still trying to play God in a young adult's life, that's spiritual abuse. An extreme case would be a father who tells his daughter, 'God told me you shouldn't marry so-and-so.' "

Host: "Then what's passive abuse, Dr. Hemfelt?"

Dr. Hemfelt: "Abandonment: death, divorce, extended separation; where the child is fostered out, or farmed out to relatives; when one of the parents is in extended military service with little or no visitation; or a two-career marriage in which the child is farmed out to daycare more than twenty hours a week from birth to age six."

Host: "Often that can't be helped."

Dr. Hemfelt: "That's exactly right. The child's head may even understand it can't be helped, but in the child's heart, it's abuse all the same. 'They went off and left me,' the child feels. The feeling has to be dealt with. It can be dealt with."

Host: "And then there's plain old neglect."

Dr. Hemfelt: "Neglect. A parent is married to someone or

something outside the family. Dad is married to his to job or to the golf course. Mom is into excessive church work, or a romantic affair. That parent's capacity to attend to kids is compromised. Illness—chronic anxiety, chronic depression—or addictions: Again, each limits the parent's nurturing capacity."

Host: "Can these abuses be unknowingly passed from generation to generation?"

Dr. Hemfelt: "Yes, for example, one woman couldn't see any abuse in her family-of-origin. 'My parents loved me and cared for me,' she said. And that was true. But her grandmother had died of TB, and her mother had an extreme obsessive-compulsive preoccupation with germs and cleanliness, an intense fear of germs, of catching disease. She was constantly disinfecting and sterilizing the bathroom—every room of the house. This young woman grew up under that. She missed a lot of time, attention, affection, and nurturing. Her mother loved her and cared for her, yes, but there are only twenty-four hours in a day, and the girl wasn't getting much of it. Her mom was too busy watching for germs."

Host: "Neglect."

Dr. Hemfelt: "Neglect. It's also neglect when one parent is undemonstrative or emotionally unavailable. A parent who never showed or expressed feelings."

Host: "It's a common male pattern in America: a father not being in touch with feelings."

Hemfelt: "So the parent can't connect with the child. Also, there's the classic codependent, the parent trying to fix an addicted spouse. It leaves little time for the kids."

Host: "Spouse of an alcoholic, for example."

Dr. Hemfelt: "Exactly. Or a man, for instance, whose mother was diagnosed with cancer when he was ten. She died when he was fifteen. His dad and mom were both absorbed in the illness. Dad tried to ease Mom's pain, help Mom; but Dad was compensating for his dying spouse. Consequently, the kids experienced a great deal of neglect. This particular man became a parent to his siblings."

Host: "When we were talking before air time you said something about blueprints."

Dr. Hemfelt: "That's a source of problems, yes. Failure of the family blueprint. If my mom and dad didn't have a good marriage and work through their own problems to find genuine intimacy, that becomes the template, the blueprint, the prototype for my marriage as an adult.

"It's not just obvious things, although those are important. But . . . for example, a man's family-of-origin may hand down the blueprint that men have permission to have affairs outside marriage. The adult male child then might compulsively act that out, even though intellectually he has other values. If push comes to shove, we tend to fall back on the blueprint, compulsively and unconsciously."

Host: "You're saying we're programmed and don't have any choice?"

Dr. Hemfelt: "Not at all. I said 'fall back on.' We have God-given choices. But our awareness of those choices may be obscured unless we are aware of the old blueprints. It can be much more subtle than having no choice. Let's take a situation common to parents in the Third Passage. The couples' marriage may be fine on the surface, but by the Third Passage, their sexuality sort of shuts down. The special bonding isn't there. The kids growing up may never see an overt indication, but they feel it. The blueprint is laid down. If Mom and Dad are not well wedded—welded—the kids sense that.

"Family blueprints are transmitted not at the intellectual level but through the emotions. That makes the blueprints very difficult to access from the intellect. They're very difficult to deal with in therapy because they don't respond to intellectual confrontation alone, though that's the place to start."

Host: "Then how do you do it, Dr. Hemfelt?"

Dr. Hemfelt: "Work around the intellect on the emotional and physical levels. We encourage couples in therapy to release pent up anger or sadness or fear from what was missing in their families of origin. When we work with a couple who cannot bond or come together because of enmeshment or estrangement, we ask them to do physical, task-oriented bonding exercises."

Host: "For example."

Dr. Hemfelt: "Well, uh . . . for example. Here are partners who are literally out of touch with each other. Their sexuality is drifting away. We assign them to spend a certain amount of time each week physically touching and pleasuring each other in a nurturing, nonsexual way."

Host: "Nonsexual?"

Dr. Hemfelt: "A back rub, massage the feet or hands. This allows physical bonding to take place at a presexual level, and it can build toward better sex and intimacy. In some cases, we assign some challenging task for the couples to do together. Maybe for a couple who never camped out, we'll ask them to do it as a couples project. Something so they have to work together as a team."

Host: "Sounds like an invitation to a divorce."

Dr. Hemfelt: (Laughs.) "It prevents one. We had a husband in the Third Passage who was tyrannical. He wasn't physically abusive, but he was abusively authoritative and always had to have his wife with him at home. On the rare occasion he went out of town, she had to check in with him, or he'd call her. It wasn't romantic jealousy. He trusted her fidelity. It was the sense that 'I have to be together with this person.' To him, it was not okay for her to be alone. So we gave them an assigment for their forthcoming vacation: rock climbing. They loved it. It was so challenging it developed strong teamwork bonding. As a result, the husband found he could begin to give his wife more autonomy. And she was able to demand it more. He could let go on control issues because they could trust the bond better."

Host: "That sounds like a contradiction in terms."

Dr. Hemfelt: "It is. It's a paradox in a way, but it's how the emotions work. The deeper and more solid the bond between man and wife, the more they can let each other go—not impose restrictive control or codependent attention."

Host: "If the bond is deep, you can let go on the surface. I see. Like the man you just described. And if Mom and Dad didn't have that in the family-of-origin then the kids don't have it?"

Dr. Hemfelt: "Exactly. And they have difficulty finding it. In war, men who go through battle together never forget the names and faces of people they fought with. Challenge, especially physical challenge, forges bonds."

In that interview Dr. Hemfelt went on to describe another sort of passive abuse, the upside-down family. This is emotional incest—when, overtly, the parent puts more responsibility on the children than they are prepared for—making them a parent to other siblings or even to the parents themselves. Dr. Hemfelt pointed out that adult-children who experienced emotional incest in the family-of-origin do more than just assume a parenting role in childhood. They may also take on the distorted role of being either the parent or the child to their spouse when they grow up and marry.

Dr. Hemfelt talked of one spouse slipping into becoming an irresponsible, irascible child, while the other spouse slips into the role of caretaker and rescuer. In the case he cited, the husband had been a responsible, productive breadwinner during Marriage Passages One and Two. The wife also had a sales career. By the Third Passage, the husband became more and more passive about his work, bringing in less money. The less he worked, the more his wife did. Soon, the wife had taken on the role of the providing parent, and her husband, that of the dependent child. Early in their marriage she'd helped him make decisions about his wardrobe. Now, she was picking his clothes and laying them out on the bed for him each morning. They would both chuckle, thinking it was kind of cute. And yet this was another mother-son subtlety.

We learned in counseling they were perfectly, malignantly matched. She had grown up in an emotionally incestuous family where the mother was chronically depressed. She had been a caregiver to her own mother, just as she was now becoming the caregiver to her husband. The husband, too, was reverting to old family patterns. He had grown up under such rigid standards, he had never been allowed to be a child. He had been given an adult behavior standard and adult expectations. Now he was rebelling, becoming the child he had never been. He would put on his suit, ostensibly to go talk to clients, and instead would take off his tie and shoot pool all day. His behavior was childish, escapist. His burned-out wife, disgusted by what their lives had become, was the one who initiated counseling.

These and other factors can drive a couple down one side or the other of the codependency wheel. How can you determine if you and your spouse have slid counterclockwise down the overly dependent side?

Exaggerated Dependence

We invite you to go down through this series of reflective statements to see if your marriage is hampered by exaggerated dependence. Do you find yourself in any of them?

_____ "I am constantly trying to please and win the favor of my spouse, even if that means burying my own feelings or compromising my own values, beliefs, and attitudes."

_____ "I push for my spouse to always agree with me." (Be honest; the push for agreement or conformity can be overt or very subtle but nonetheless powerful.)

_____ "My mood swings (up and down both) are tied directly to those of my spouse."

_____ "Our sexual sharing has become routine and overly predictable." (Has it become so routine and devoid of excitement that your sex relationship has diminished or faded to nonexistence?)

_____ "Either I or my spouse has come to function as a chronic therapist or counselor (rescuer) to the other."

_____ "One of us has assumed a chronic sick role (physically, mentally, or emotionally) which requires the constant attention or intervention from the spouse."

_____ "I have placed my spouse on an unrealistic pedestal."

_____ "My spouse has placed me on such a pedestal."

_____ "I experience withdrawal symptoms when I am out of the presence of my spouse?" (If there are brief separations due to work, travel, or such, do you feel a vague anxiety about these times of separation? Have you placed unreasonable demands on your spouse to curtail outside activities as a means of trying to ease that anxiety?)

_____ "I experience unreasonable fears about the status of my spouse's romantic and sexual fidelity."

_____ "I have gradually become a clone of my spouse." (Do you sometimes wonder whether you even know your own thoughts, opinions, values, and feelings apart from those you mimic and mirror in each other?)

_____ "The prospect of a life apart from my spouse (such as a circumstance of premature death) overwhelms me with feelings of terror and insecurity."

If you discover yourself checking several of these statements, consider it an indication that, for you, codependent tendencies may be present and reaching a problem level. You may be traveling down the wheel counterclockwise.

This exaggerated dependence is only half the picture. Let's look at that diagram of the relationship wheel again and see the other side of a marriage that's gone out of balance.

Exaggerated Independence

When the couple drifts clockwise down the wheel, their interests begin to diverge. That in itself isn't too bad. But the momentum, unchecked, carries that divergence to an extreme. Estranged, the marriage partners have almost nothing in common except irritation and friction. Brought to its full course, this estrangement becomes constant hostility, or periods of extreme hostility interspersed with periods of extreme "lovey-dovey" closeness. Both the intense closeness and the howling fights are the fruits of codependency and can occur on the same branch, to the confusion of friends and family.

Separation or divorce usually does not end this codependent relationship, though observers on the outside may think perhaps it ought to. Both persons feed on the energy of the friction, of the love-hate. The seesaw of emotions continues between this couple until one or the other realizes what's happening and resolves this independent dependency. Sometimes that never happens.

Passage Three is a time of special susceptibility to another form of exaggerated independence—growing apart. The accumulated pressures of career, homemaking, childbearing and rearing throughout Passages One, Two, and Three grow in an almost geometric fashion. By the early to middle part of Passage Three, most couples can only survive by division of labor and specialization. While Henry Ford might approve of this approach to getting the job done and moving the family down the assembly line of life, it can leave partners in Passage Three mov-

ing in separate orbits and wondering what they share besides the
same last name and the same zip code.

How about You?

Have you and your spouse begun to drift down that wheel
clockwise toward exaggerated independence? Check the statements below to see if they reflect your relationship:

_____ "Our lives (activities, interests, pursuits) have begun to
move in widely divergent directions."

_____ "I have secretly questioned why I'm staying in this relationship."

_____ "I (or my spouse) periodically threaten divorce."

_____ "One or both of us has quietly resigned from the sexual
intimacy of this marriage." (Don't limit the meaning to
the physical act here. The physical act without intimacy
or fulfillment counts as a resignation.)

_____ "Romantic affairs outside our marriage or affairs of the
heart have scarred its intimacy."

_____ "I'm not sure I even know my spouse anymore. We live
separate lives.

_____ My spouse has been consumed with someone or something outside the marriage. I feel like I've lost her (or
him).

Does each of you have a long list of accumulated resentments
about real or imagined emotional hurts experienced at the hands
of your spouse earlier in your marriage? Are these lists held up
against each other as weapons of conflict? Are the two of you
well accustomed to playing the mutual blame game ("If only
you had not. . . " "If only you would. . . ")? Check the following if they apply:

_____ "One of us has begun to be constantly critical of the
other. This person views the other through a magnifying glass that highlights every flaw and imperfection."

_____ "I have begun to think, 'I don't seem to be able to do
anything right in this marriage.' "

_____ "Our marriage has reached a point of mutual impasse
over a major issue, like deciding on a unifying team
approach to parenting the children."

_____ "I find myself living in a state of constant tension and agitation in this marriage. The moments of peace seem to be only a temporary and fleeting truce before the next inevitable eruption of conflict."

_____ "One or both of us has begun to recruit the children, extended-family members, or even mutual friends to take sides with us, enlisting them in these seemingly never-ending disputes."

We posed these questions to a couple in our marital counsel, Dave and Genie. Reflecting upon the questions, they perceived that they were drifting down the wheel clockwise to exaggerated independence. Dave came to us because his second marriage was fast headed down the same road his first marriage had taken, with disaster at its end. Dave left the ministry after six years' service for the Lord, because his wife divorced him. Three years later he returned to the pastorate and subsequently remarried. Eleven years later his new wife, Genie, began to nag him with the same complaint his first wife did: "The people in the church always come before your family. You're never here to help me with the kids. In fact, they hardly know what you look like anymore. And I'm beginning to resent spending my every minute with them." Dave was hearing the same tape he had heard in his first marriage. "Women are all alike," he fumed. "Bah!" Dave didn't realize that he was the one who had slipped back into his old patterns of workaholism.

We had to help Dave see that his marriage had become a comfortable old garment, present but unnoticed, taken for granted. Again, as in his first union, Dave had made his work— the church he pastored—more important than his family. Dave had to participate in the marriage more; he had become so meshed in his work that it absorbed most of his time and energy.

Genie had her share of the problem too. Genie and Dave had two children of their own. Lyndon, seven, was what they call hyperactive. Not naughty, just constantly in motion. He wanted to build a tree house but Genie didn't let him after he fell out of the tree the third time. Lyndon's teacher said Genie ought to have him seen by a doctor familiar with Attention Deficit Syndrome, whatever that was, because he was more disruptive than the average child. But where was Genie going to find time to take Lyndon into town for that stuff when she had to look after both kids and manage the house and their financial affairs without any help from Dave? The children were becoming an overwhelming burden rather than a joy to her.

Genie and Dave's task was to recognize the source of conflict and to rebuild a healthy interdependence in their relationship.

Healthy Interdependence

A tricky balancing act is required to stay at 12 o'clock on the codependency wheel. Clients of ours, Ramona and George had to learn that.

Ramona nodded her head as she talked about her authoritarian father. "Dad is a history professor. I have never had permission to question his opinions. Not until I was an adult," she related, "did we talk about the end of the Vietnam War. This was fifteen years after it happened. The end came in the early 1970s so this would be what? Eighty-seven? Eighty-eight? Father told me it was a mistake. 'We should have stayed until there was a decisive victory.' I disagreed, but I did so politely. I just said, 'I believe the war was going nowhere; it needed to end, victory or no victory.'

"My father was so shocked that I would disagree with him, he wouldn't speak to me for a week. A week later he sent me a note —mailed it!—explaining his position on the war question."

As Ramona moved into the Third Passage of her marriage, she began to chronically fight and find fault with her husband. The friction had started clear back at the wedding, but many distractions—buying a home, getting the kids going—had minimized Ramona's time spent with her husband George. Now that things were settling down and her husband was doing well, Ramona was becoming increasingly critical and antagonistic. When she came to us, she thought she must have picked the wrong man.

What was she afraid of? It eventually came out as she probed within herself. She really harbored deep fears of intimacy: "If I get close to a man, he will overwhelm me, and suffocate me, and consume me like Dad did."

Ramona's husband George grew up under a passive, cold, intellectually aloof father and a rigid, dogmatic mother. His parents pretended that his father was the head of the household and the main provider. But in reality, his dad was never much of a success as a salesman. His mother supported the family financially with her job as a teacher and generally acted as the head of the household. She held extreme religious views, and by the time George was an adolescent, she began to label many of his school friends as ungodly. One-by-one, she banned him from any affiliation with these friends.

George was terrified by the negative power his mother wielded in his life. He feared that he might turn out to be like his dad, never to stand his ground, always to be dominated by the woman he supposedly loved.

George, too, had been able to lay aside his inner fears during Passages One and Two, as he put together his business. But by Passage Three, as his marriage matured, he found himself picking fights with Ramona, taking a stand where no stand was needed, just to do it. Besides, it was safer than true intimacy.

Healing for this couple involved three things. First, both had to recognize where they were on the wheel. Second, they had to realize that beneath their anger lay the true motivations—fear and insecurity. Third, they had to recognize that the roots of their problem were firmly embedded in family-of-origin issues.

How About You?

You, too, if you are sliding down one side or the other of the codependency wheel, must deal with those three points.

Look again at the wheel. Where would you put yourself and your mate? If you are not very near the top, linked in a healthy interdependence, codependency may become a serious problem. It so often emerges and intensifies in this passage.

There are two ways to deal with it. Recovery is best, and it is by far best done by both partners. We strongly recommend the book *Love Is a Choice* by Dr. Robert Hemfelt, Dr. Frank Minirth, and Dr. Paul Meier (Nashville: Thomas Nelson, 1989) for detailed guidelines to help you deal effectively with codependency problems. That book spells it all out. If your partner refuses to participate, or perhaps even consider that there might be a problem, there is still much you yourself can do. You can begin coping with the problem immediately. We call the coping steps the three R's and six C's. You grasp the meaning of three R's in your life, then take six C steps of spousal detachment and recovery.

The Three R'S

If codependency (multigenerational dysfunction, if you want a fancy name) is influencing your marriage, you can rest assured it's not a positive influence. The problems you now have are a response to something painful or missing in your past. These deficiencies cause you to:

1. Repeat, re-create, and restage in your own marriage those old problems from your parents' or grandparents' marriage;

2. Rebel and go blindly in the opposite direction that your family-of-origin pursued; and/or

3. Redeem somehow what was painful or shameful in that original family, or try to.

A client, Donald, in our counsel illustrates these three R's vividly. He was in the Third Passage, the father of three elementary-school children. He came to us, not for marriage therapy but for financial counseling.

A dynamic lawyer, Donald's workaholism had allowed him to become partner at the law firm by an early age. His take-home pay had jumped astronomically during his twelve-year career. Yet in spite of his successes, Donald was in dire financial straits. Never content to save or invest cautiously, he repeatedly poured his money into high-risk investment strategies in real estate, the stock market, and start-up business ventures. Each new investment scheme promised instant wealth. But as each new venture backfired, instead, Donald not only lost his original investment but also went deeper into debt.

As we helped Donald tackle the emotional factors triggering his financial distress, we found he also had problems in his marriage. He had promised his wife, Toni, an endless number of times that this would be the last time he would borrow or invest. But he continued to break his vows and would even lie to Toni about his financial transactions.

Although he was the breadwinner, the roller coaster of the financial losses and gains and growing debt left his family in a financial bind. Toni had to work part-time in nursing, though she hated to—she wanted to be home with her kids instead of at work.

By picking apart his early life he came up with this picture. His father was highly competitive. He pushed his two boys and three girls for maximum athletic performance. Donald could not remember a time or circumstance when the father was emotionally available to his sons and daughters. He overinvolved himself in their lives, but only as a coach. Detached from their lives, he didn't know them well.

Donald ended up practicing all three R's in his own adult life. In one way, he repeatedly REPLICATED the high performance standards his father had so vigorously pushed. When Donald signed with a law firm, he came on like gangbusters, proving himself quickly and well. His quest for instant wealth was also his attempt to prove himself financially to his father.

Donald also REBELLED against those same excessive performance expectations. He could never really please Dad; he never made peace with that unresolved need. (It didn't help that he had scant natural athletic ability). He could never earn love or affection. The rebellion emerged in two ways—first, through his risky investments. This pattern was not only an effort to prove himself to his father but, ironically, a means of sabotaging that success, of throwing away the success he was attempting to earn.

In his head, Donald knew better than to repeat his father's mistakes. He could see it coming and couldn't stop it. That was his self-sabotage, his sit-down strike against his father, the part of him that never bought into Dad's performance requirement. It was his unconscious way of saying, "If I can't live up to your standards, I'll live down to my own self-imposed failure." It was his way of expressing anger at the highly conditional love his father imposed.

Donald's rebellion also came out in his family life. He superficially appeared to be a superhusband (there were those standards again), overinvolved in family activities, doting on his wife. Deeply hidden was another cry: "I don't want to support this family." Certainly he would never say that consciously to himself or to his wife. So he unconsciously moved his family into the position where his wife had to move from part-time to full-time nursing.

Finally, he tried to REDEEM everything wrong in the past. There was his low self-esteem born of Dad's treatment. Dad, of course, didn't feel very good about himself, either. Now Donald was taking on Dad's insecurity from the prior generation. Too, he tried to redeem Dad's shortcomings by becoming over involved with his own kids. He was the PTA president, the scout master, the team coach, the Sunday school teacher, the perfect father. He was trying to be it all—the father his own father had never been.

Donald's rebellion was burning him out. Part of his present emotional crisis was from sheer exhaustion. He couldn't super-achieve on the job and on parenting and on coaching and such.

Although his sex life had diminished greatly, he had not come in for sex therapy. But his pattern of pushing himself very hard, then sloughing off, was spilling over into his private life. His wife, Toni, understandably struggling with deep anger, had to learn the six C's of spouse recovery for living with a dysfunctional person. The first three work within the self, and the second three are active steps of loving detachment. All are healthy reminders she had to give herself.

The Two Sets of Three C's

First C: I did not CAUSE the problem. Toni felt guilt about pushing him so hard, or putting excessive financial expectations on him, and she blamed herself for his intensity. When he made irresponsible investments, she blamed herself for not encouraging and nurturing him more. She labored under the fiction that she generated these extremes in her man. For Toni, it was just plain liberating when she realized she need not take responsibility for Donald's overperformance on the job and irresponsibility with their finances. It all came from his background, not from Toni.

Second C: I cannot CURE.

She also found it liberating that she didn't have to be his therapist. In his depressions she spent hours trying to talk him out of them. Partway through his therapy, she sent him a resignation letter. No more therapy. Plenty of listening, but no more attempts to fix his problems.

Third C: I may not even CONTROL it.

No more magical thinking, either. She discovered she was trying to be outrageously frugal with her household budget to make him more responsible with their assets. Then she'd earn money to bring down the financial pressure on him, but that never seemed to do it. It certainly didn't bring down the pressures he put on himself. Any change in her wasn't going to cure him.

She also recognized she couldn't control his problems precisely because they didn't come from her. Much as she tried to fine-tune his performance, encouraging him to slow down his workaholism or be more conservative with his investments, the pattern repeated itself anyway.

She obtained great freedom from those three C's. She also tackled the three C's of active steps of detachment a spouse can take.

First C: CONFRONT and CHALLENGE the dysfunction I see.

Toni didn't nag, although heaven knows it was tempting. When she saw the destructive pattern of making money and losing money begin its spiral, she gave herself permission to firmly and lovingly confront Donald. Once a week as things progressed, she sat down in a calm moment and told him what she saw. "I'm concerned. I see you overextended and overindulging yourself in our kids' lives. I see your money pattern starting again."

Second C: CEASE enabling behaviors. Maybe Toni couldn't control the situation, but she could avoid becoming a co-conspirator, a co-participant in Donald's dysfunction. She had to give herself permission to do this, over and over. Before, when he overscheduled she would make excuses for him. She quit that. She quit excusing him away to family members. When he lost a large sum of money, she used to make her own rationalization or recited his party line. Now she said, simply, "I don't know. Ask Donald about that." Never did she violate a confidence but neither did she cover for him.

Third C: I can CHANGE me. And if I change, the relationship cannot stay the same; it will also change. She changed herself by first realizing she had grown up under a workaholic father, and had doubtless been shaped—or misshaped—by that. Quite probably her initial attraction to Donald subconsciously involved, "I couldn't fix Dad, so I'll fix Donald, who is like my Dad. If I just love him enough I can fix him." She was wrapped up in her own three R's, restaging the same pain when Donald neglected her that she had felt when pushed aside by her father.

Donald was either married to his job when at the high end of his roller coaster, or flat and depressed when at the low end of the money-made/money-lost cycle.

By working out the problems of her own family-of-origin pain and grieving, she strengthened herself to do those other C's better. She began, too, to get a new sense of identity that did not depend on either Dad's approval or Donald's. She had always somehow felt that if she got stronger it would threaten her marriage. She discovered quite the opposite. As she gained more personal identity, it strengthened the union.

Rebuild Your Personal Identity

Recall the case of Genie and Dave—where Dave was immersed in his pastoral duties at the expense of his family. Genie was left holding the bag; she had to do everything, neglecting her own needs. As Toni had done, Genie had to develop her own interests, her own identity again. She needed to see herself as someone besides a mother and pastor's wife. We helped her shore up her image of herself.

Genie was savvy enough to realize that resentment bears no good fruit. It changes nothing. It poisons only the waters of the person whom it fills. Unwilling to let her resentment grow, and not quite ready to lock the kids in a closet for the next ten years, she chose the third option—carve out a bit of time and effort for herself. We helped her sit down and write out a plan.

Look at the Whole Picture

Genie's plan, subdivided, got the kids through high school and listed the graduation dates. She listed emancipation dates: when each child got a driver's license and no longer had to be chauffeured. Suddenly she could see the light at the end of the tunnel. This hectic child-care schedule wouldn't last forever. It only seemed that way.

She listed projects she wanted to complete or begin, projects having nothing to do with kids or Dave or the pastorate. She wanted to finish the afghan she started in sewing class in high school, when she learned to crochet. She wanted to make a really nice nativity set, all handmade with stiffened fabrics and porcelain faces and hands; she'd saved all the patterns and instructions she found four years ago.

Finally, she began a calendar of hope, a grid covering the next sixteen years. On it she planned what she would do for herself, year by year, as the kids grew up, and the ages they would be when she did these things.

Don't Neglect Yourself

As for the present, Genie could afford a baby-sitter three hours a week. Then, happily, eagerly, she began creating her nativity set, a few hours at a time. A whole delicious block of free time just for her. No kids, no telephone, no bother.

She spent time also simply dealing with the resentment. She eventually had to make peace with the burden of responsibility for the children. Because of her light-at-the-end-of-the-tunnel list, she could manage that well enough.

She deliberately made peace with the sacrifices she had to make for the kids. Sacrifices were inevitable. She grieved losses and steeled herself for the future. Sacrificial living wasn't over yet. In fact, it would probably never end completely.

Genie probably never noticed, but her expanded interests brightened her outlook and even, to an extent, her personality. Dave noticed the change, although he took a long time realizing that some stiff brocade and a few porcelain heads would make a difference.

How About You?

What are some things you've dreamed of doing? Try listing at least three (for example, finishing my college degree at night school):

1. _____
2. _____
3. _____

What on this list must wait until the kids are grown (for example, attending classes on a full-time basis)?

1. _____
2. _____

What might you do now? If there's nothing here you could do for yourself now, can you think of something else that you could use as time to yourself (for example, setting time each

day to read privately and taking one summer course when the
kids are away at camp)?_____
_____

Genie resented the fact that Dave was so busy caring for the
parishioners of his church that he slighted his parental duties.
She did not learn until they entered counseling that Dave resented the time and attention she lavished on the kids instead of
him. He felt not so much jealous as neglected.

Genie's full identity had become enmeshed in motherhood
and preacher's-wifehood. There was too little Genie left for happiness. With cases like Genie, we might invite both spouses to
draw a series of pie charts to show where they think their time
goes. Then we ask that they draw charts to show where they
would like the time to go.

How About You?

Draw a simple pie chart. Divide the pie into sections corresponding to where you put most of your time and effort. An
example of how Genie's pie looked is below. She got to bed
around 11 and was up at 6, which left 18 hours out of 24 to use.
As you can see, nearly 75% of her waking time was directly devoted to child-care—carpooling to events, helping with homework, volunteering at school, or indirectly associated—naptime
for her preschooler, for example. That left 25%, about 4 hours,
of which 2 were invariably eaten up by the demands of running
the household on her own and by her duties as a pastor's wife.
Draw your pie now. Be honest about where your time is really
spent.

Now draw a pie showing where you would like your precious
time to go. Put down those dreams you have for yourself—
looking back at the dreams you listed above. What are those
dreams you can pursue now, even with kids, the house, and
maybe a job? Genie's dream pie chart looked very different than
her other chart. What about yours?

We try to help a person restructure their boundaries, priorities, and schedules to come closer to their dream pie chart. This
helps both the workaholic and the overloaded mother.

Another way to do this exercise is to list the things that take
your time, with the most time-consuming items first. The physi-

Genie's Time Chart

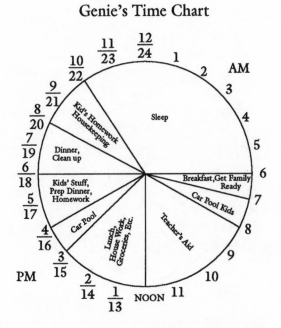

Your Time Chart

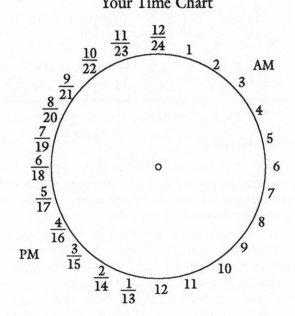

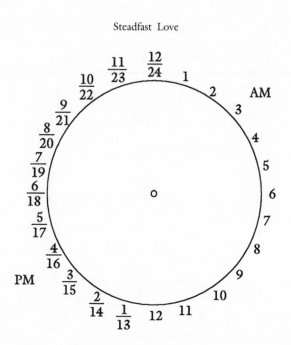

Your Dream Pie Chart

cal ink-on-paper list also helps you to literally see the problem. Rearranging the list is then another visual aid to solving priority and boundary problems.

Genie had to reforge her self, reestablishing her own identity apart from all the demands and circumstances around her. Dave had to recast his identity as a husband and father. This made it much easier for them to balance at the top of the wheel.

How to Stay Balanced

As Frank Minirth explains, "The goal in marriage is healthy interdependence. A great mistake is when one partner tries to feel all the feelings (or do everything) in the marriage. Those persons feel everything so intensely, they cannot live without the other person. This leaves the other person feeling inferior. The other extreme is also a mistake, and we see it frequently in the clinic. That's when the person shuts down and lets the spouse do all the feeling (or do everything). God doesn't want you turning everything over to another person.

"We're not saying dependency is bad. Healthy dependency is excellent. Be dependent on God, on friends; that's okay in itself. You have to watch out for the danger of codependency. And incidentally, divorce never cures codependency. The problem lies below the level of the marriage, deep inside the individual."

Picture if you will, a one-legged sitting stool. You may have seen it in encyclopedias or in actual use. It looks like a kind of walking stick, something a proper gentleman would take out on a stroll through the park. When the gentleman wishes to sit down he unfolds the top of his walking stick into a seat of sorts and there perches, his weight firmly supported. It looks uncomfortable and tipsy, but actually it's not.

Geometry buffs understand why a stool sits best on three legs; three points define a plane. They can also define a stable marriage. A four-legged stool or table will wobble if all four legs are not exactly even and sitting on a flat surface—as evidenced by the number of folded matchbooks under restaurant tables. Likewise, a one- or two-legged stool cannot stand alone. But you can perch a three-legged stool on uneven ground and sit securely. You can tip a three-legged stool forward while you're milking, the better to manage a bored cow who's finished eating. A three-legged stool adapts solidly to any situation.

Every marriage exists as a three-legged stool. One leg is the husband; another is the wife. The third leg changes through time: it might be the kids, as was the case for Genie; or the job; or buying and furnishing a home. But eventually, the kids leave home. Retirement ends the job. The house is sold. Suddenly, the stool's remaining two legs only have each other. That prospect terrifies many couples in their Third Passage of marriage.

"I remember," one of our clients recalled, "the night before our youngest child went to college. I sat on the sofa looking across the room at my husband in his lazy boy, and I thought to myself, *'What in heaven's name will we ever talk about when the kids are gone? Do we have anything in common besides them?'*"

To use the principle that a solid stool requires three sound, sturdy legs; not one or two strong ones with one or two spindly ones; the challenge in this Third Passage of marriage is to build and maintain those three legs. The couple must make sure that two legs (each other) are equally as strong. They also must learn to build a strong third leg.

Maintaining personal identity by avoiding the codependency drift is one way to shore up two legs of the marriage stool. But it is only one of the tasks this Third Passage requires. To prevent yourself from becoming stuck in the Third Passage, you must consider others too. One of them is saying good-bye to the past which is never an easy thing to do.

Chapter 3

Can You Say Good-bye?

S uch a sad word, good-bye. . . . Not always! Good-byes said at partings are sad because the parting is sad. The good-bye itself is nothing more than a herald of change, sometimes good and sometimes bad. Many times it is only by saying good-bye to one thing that can you embrace another. You must put down the pen in your hand if you wish to pick up the pencil. That is what good-bye is about—change. For every good-bye there is a hello. Developing the skill to say good-bye gracefully can be good for your marriage. That skill has not been honed, because you have not yet realized your need to say good-bye until about this third passage.

The Second Task: Say the Final Good-Byes

Some important good-byes must be said in this passage of marriage, and you have finally reached the stage of life in which you are mature enough to say them well. You will be putting away the instability of extreme youth ("But I'm still young!" you wail. To which we reply, "Would you *really* want to go back to those uncertain, confusing, wrenching teen years?") That's not a bad good-bye, for the hello accompanying it greets wisdom and security.

51

Still, embers of that teenage fire remain. Deep within each human heart lurks the yearning that somewhere, someone is waiting to step in and direct you in all the right moves. You want a "god" to take over. Because the human heart embraces the tangible and the real so much more easily than the intangible, it substitutes your parents as god. Why, it took you over a decade as you were growing up just to realize that your parents weren't perfect. The ancient childhood dream of perfect parents acting with godlike wisdom lingers on, and for good reason. This was the beginning of your search for God, the taste of God that whets your appetite.

Say Good-bye to Your Parents

Parents provide an important safety net while the kids are growing up. That buffer against life is hard to shed. A healthy friendship in which the parent is no longer a primary authority figure is not the same as the original parent-child relationship. Delightful and rewarding as the new friendship may be, the past must be grieved and put behind.

What If Your Parents Are Unavailable?

Let us first assume that your parents are either deceased or physically unavailable for some reason. Perhaps a parent, suffering from Alzheimers or a stroke, or some similar problem, can no longer make coherent contact with you. If you are an adoptee, you have two sets of parents to say good-bye to: your biological parents and your adoptive parents. Write each deceased or unavailable parent a letter, or record a cassette tape. You may want to do this in your journal, if you have one. Consider including the following in your letter:

- Tell of some high points of your memories with them, acknowledging the huge part they played in your life.
- Tell of some values of theirs that you've adopted as your own, thus acknowledging their leadership in your life.
- Tell them of your love as a child to a parent, identifying the emotional bond between you.
- Forgive them their failures and imperfections. As humans they are bound to have them. Be as specific as you can.

- Say good-bye to the person you have just summarized. Say the words aloud, write them down, and look at them.
- Reassure them (and yourself) that you are now fully an adult, and remind them specifically of some new ways you are assuming greater adult authority and responsibility in your own life.

Picture the person in your mind. If, as with an unknown biological parent, you have no visual memories of your parent, set your mind on any of the guesswork pictures you formed through your life of what they might have been like. In that case you are saying good-bye to your perception of your parent as much as you are saying good-bye to your actual parent.

Lay your hands flat on the letter, touching it, claiming it in lieu of the person, and pray to God on that person's behalf. Give thanks for that parent's influence in your life. Incidentally, bad influences are never entirely negative; the most destructive influence still shapes you in some positive way as well. For example, a child neglected during the school years develops a strong sense of self-reliance which proves valuable when the child reaches adulthood.

Now, finally, picture in your mind's eye waving good-bye to that person and walking away from him or her. You may want to include a special word of prayer, asking God to empower you to make this final journey into adulthood and to relinquish the lost remnants of the emotional umbilical cord.

If Your Parents Are Available

If your parent(s) are living and available, go through exactly this same exercise, right up to the final picture of you walking away. Now, you cannot just walk away from your living parents. Neither are they likely to understand should you step up to them and say good-bye. So in your mind's eye, now, turn around. Picture yourself walking back to them. Place them on equal footing with any other valued companion. "Hello, friend."

It may take a while, if you are in frequent contact with your parents, to get your heart to accept the good-bye. Remember that changing our words and actions can change our feelings. In word and deed treat your parents with no less respect, no less love, but as friends, not demi-gods. Remember, you are entering a new peer-to-peer relationship with your parents.

Failing to say good-bye to your parents with heart as well as mind is a sure way to get stuck in this passage. As Susan Hemfelt says, "You can't get anywhere focusing on the now in addition to the past. You have to focus on the now and the future." That includes your focus on yourself as a son/daughter of someone, not as a child.

This passage, then, brackets the age when you can put the childhood dream behind you. No white knight, no perfect parent, not even God will make your choices for you and clear your path. Now it is time for you to acknowledge the truth behind one other good-bye: There is no security here on earth.

Say Good-bye to Earthly Security

One of our friends and her husband began to invest in the stock market during this Third Passage of marriage. They were preparing for the future—for the education of their children and their eventual retirement.

Our friend began watching the stock market. Each day she would turn to the financial section of the newspaper to read the report of their stocks. Were they up an eighth? Down a half? In the next year their stocks went up a few times, and down more frequently.

"I can remember when it hit me," this friend recalls. "I was driving to the grocery store after reading the morning paper. All of a sudden the obvious struck me: none of those stocks were completely safe. There was no place we could put our money and know without doubt it would be there for us. No savings and loan association, no bank, no investment was absolutely secure. There was no guarantee of anything lasting until tomorrow. Whatever we had and whatever we did, we had it and did it by the grace of God."

Your security blanket—whatever your security symbols are—has worn threadbare. Here now, at last, the illusion of security rips asunder. A key factor in this Third Passage is realizing that no human institution and no one human being has ultimate power. That power rests ultimately with God.

For help in time of strife, pain, and chaos, people in the Alcoholics Anonymous recovery program call upon a higher power for their understanding. At the Minirth-Meier Clinics, and in our own lives, we take that action two steps further, as we outline in *Path to Serenity* (Nashville: Thomas Nelson, 1991) and *Steps to a New Beginning* (Nashville: Thomas Nelson, 1992). We identify the higher power as the God of Abraham, Isaac, and Jacob, the Father and His Son Jesus Christ. And we don't wait for recovery to make Him the third leg of our marriage stool.

The solid marriages, the stable relationships, all establish God as the third leg early on. This does not mean that if you have not, and you've already been married many years, that it is too late. It is never too late. But why procrastinate on a good thing if you have not made that choice yet?

We do not mean giving lip service to God, or tossing in the saying of grace at meals, or church attendance, or Bible reading. Each of those things in its place is very important. But none of them by itself makes God the center of your life and marriage. Those things proceed out of your relationship with the living God.

Each of us individually has recognized, in one way or another, that we have fallen short of the standards God requires. All men and women do. We each came to understand that our shortfall had to be paid for, either with our own blood of life, or a substitute's. We each acknowledge that substitute was Jesus Christ, and by His death our shortfall is taken care of. We can now face God, not because of our own excellence but because of Jesus Christ's sacrifice.

Once we became God's, we took one more step. We let God guide what we do, through His word and occasionally through His direct intervention. He is the CEO of our marriages and our lives. The pilot of our vessel. We deliberately ask Him to become the third leg of our marriage stool, the pillar of our union.

Susan Hemfelt points out, "We have to look to God for healing and strength, not each other. Only God knows us well enough to keep us growing in synch with Him."

Mary Alice adds this regarding her reliance upon Christ. "When it came to role models; examples of the way to live right and live well; I was blessed by my grandparents and parents. Mom and Daddy were married forty-four years before he died.

They were such loving, giving people. But Christ, of course, is the ultimate example of how to live. Christ will never leave us. He is the basis of all of what Frank and I want to share with other people. It's not what we humans do, it's what Christ did."

Reliance upon Christ is the pillar that forms the only lasting mainstay of marriage. But what about other false securities?

Say Good-bye to the Illusions (and Say Hello to the Healthy Disillusionment)

Not even love and intimacy represent absolute security. Your spouse can't be god to you. And that's another realization that hits you in this Third Passage of marriage. The white knight or beautiful princess does not exist, and often that disillusionment can stall a marriage and lock it into a passage.

The roots of disillusionment lie within our hidden fears. Thus, identifying your fears and dragging them out into the open is a means of working through the disillusionment.

Mary Alice knows about fear firsthand. "Fear attacks every area of our lives now and then. Especially when we find ourselves fearing the passages that are coming—the empty nest coming, or circumstances you know are coming. We might be fearful that it won't be perfect, whatever 'it' is at the moment.

"I've seen fear debilitate women in how they raise their kids, how they respond to their husband; it just wipes out their daily functions.

"Control issues, too, are based on fear. I've seen my daughter's friends so tightly controlled at home that they can't grow. A mother can be so domineering, she can't talk about kid things or accept the kid's point of view. It's fear; fear that the kid won't be perfect, or won't have perfect influences around that cause the mother's dominance.

"And fear of the unknown *really* takes us off the path to our God."

Adding to the fears that come as a natural part of this Third Passage are the fears basic to anyone at anytime: fears of rejection, of not being acceptable to our spouse or to our God. Every person must look courageously at himself or herself for, frankly, a lot of that fear is legitimate. We are all imperfect people. No person is acceptable to God as is. He accepts that person through the mediation of Jesus. And yet, once the man or woman comes to terms with imperfection, knowing that in many ways he or she is unacceptable, that person is able to accept his or her spouse's imperfections more realistically and tolerance grows.

Unconditional acceptance, while not possible in its pure form for mortal human beings, is a positive goal for marriage partners. Once you come to love and cherish the true person in your spouse, you have the freedom to relax and let down your own facade. It removes the stress we put on ourselves. And, one less stress to deal with lifts a great load off our shoulders. We can then begin to rebuild our relationship.

Say Hello to Intimacy

Think again about the incident in James and Lonna Jorgenson's lives when their two-year-old Joci died. Both of them were so wrapped up in the children, and in the medical emergency, there was no time left for just the two of them to be together. The glib and useless admonition "make time for each other" simply would not serve. Very often in every couple's life, time together falls by the wayside like that. It happens a lot, especially in this Third Passage.

What robs the togetherness in your life? Think about everything that drives a wedge, however slight, between you and your mate. What are the roots of your conflicts? The deep ones? Think too about everything that draws you together. Avoid passing judgments about what should or shouldn't pull us and draw us. This is strictly an evaluation of what works or doesn't work in our present intimacy. Write them down in a list like the following. Add more of your own if you need to.

Things That Pull Us Apart

1. The Kids
2. Our Jobs
3. Our Finances
4. My Parents
5. His/Her Parents

   6. _____
   7. _____
   8. _____
   9. _____
10. _____

Things That Draw Us Together

1. Our Religion
2. Family Crises
3. The Kids
4. Our Friends
5. Our Home
6. _____
7. _____
8. _____
9. _____
10. _____

Looking back over these two lists, can you see which things you can capitalize on to find common ground? Talk about them. In so doing, you will build intimacy in your relationship.

Resolving conflict is a crucial tool for building intimacy in your relationship and minimizing issues that wedge between you and your spouse.

Say Hello to Conflict

"I already did that, by getting married. I said hello to a lot of conflict!"

By now, you've become so accustomed to your mate that, at least on the surface, you've quit talking to each other. We mean, *really* talking. Getting the point across. Hot words fly, and loving words purr, but real communication may not be happening. A major part of completing the tasks of the Third Passage—all the tasks—involves breaking the old patterns of communication and building new ones.

Consider Rick and Nancy, the couple playing Pictionary℗ at the close of Chapter one. Nancy could predict what Rick would say. Even before the question was asked she knew what the answer would be. She didn't have to talk to him anymore. She knew in advance what he'd say, what he'd think. And so she didn't bother talking anymore.

In no area of marital concern does this rote predictability and lack of communication show up more than in conflict. Nancy could tell you what they would fight about. She could tell you what the same stale arguments would be, on either side. She and Rick are fairly typical of couples in this passage.

By the time a couple has reached their Third Passage of Marriage, conflict issues have arisen time and time again. In theory, the partners should have learned to deal with them by now. The fact is, many third-passage spouses have not, because they no longer even hear what's *really* going on anymore. Many third-passage spouses joke that they can anticipate unresolved arguments so well they could assign a number to each one and call out the number as each issue arises rather than fight about it.

In healthy situations, the resolution of the conflict has strengthened intimacy. Too often, though, conflict management in this Third Passage involves other not-so-healthy methods—squelching the argument for the kids' sake, ignoring conflict until it either eats you up inside or explodes, or, fighting it out tooth and nail. Spouses locked into not-so-healthy situations either drift apart or deliberately shove each other apart.

The challenge is to use conflict management to open up real expression between spouses, to the immense benefit of the marriage. This happens only if the couple practices good conflict-resolution skills.

Frank Minirth explains, "Resolving conflict and strengthening intimacy are not two separate processes. Three important things happen when a couple truly and completely resolve a conflict:

"First, the conflict is completed. It won't rear its ugly head again in the union. Think how easily unresolved conflicts just keep resurfacing every time friction develops. That cycle of acrimony breaks when the conflict is dissolved.

"Secondly, each person understands himself or herself better. 'Why did I get into this fight, anyway? What are my deep down motivations and attitudes? Should they be adjusted?' That introspection will serve the person well the next time conflict arises either inside or outside the marriage.

"Thirdly, the couple know each other better. And, that is the very heart of oneness. Done properly and well, therefore, crisis and conflict resolution encourage intimacy."

Before you can resolve a conflict, you have to know what it is. And by now, you and your spouse are aware of all the causes of conflict in your lives, right? Maybe. Remember, you may not have been truly talking to each other for quite some time.

Review again the "Things That Pull Us Apart and Draw Us Together" lists above. This time jot a few words to reflect a recent conflict between you and your spouse that arose regarding each topic. Count both running conflicts that keep showing up again and again, and single-time blow-ups. If you can't remember any conflict on that subject, fine. Continue to the next. Hardly anybody fights about everything.

1. The Kids, The Conflict:_____

_____

2. Our Jobs, The Conflict:_____

_____

3. Our Finances, The Conflict:_____

_____

_____

_____

4. My Parents, The Conflict:_____

_____

5. My In-laws, The Conflict:_____

_____

6. Our Religion, The Conflict:_____

_____

7. Our Friends, The Conflict:_____

_____

8. Our Home, The Conflict:_____

_____

9._____

_____

10._____

_____

You have just identified a lot of symptoms of conflict. Now let's get down to analyzing the real causes of conflict.

Causes and Symptoms

Boy, do you feel rotten! Sneezing, a runny nose sore from so much blowing, no energy, aching all over. . . You take cold medicine, but unlike many medications, cold medicine does nothing to cure the cold. All the king's horses and all the king's men have not been able to cure the common cold. The medicine alleviates the symptoms somewhat—the nose does not run so fast, the sneezing lessens, the aches abate. But the cold virus, follows its merry course unhindered.

The germs cause the symptoms. Instead of that nasty cold, should you contract one of certain treatable kinds of pneumonia, the appropriate antibiotics will stop the cause—the pneumococcus germ—and thereby the symptoms as well.

Married couples assume that conflict in their union causes separation. Actually, conflict is usually not a cause; it's a symptom. The wedge has already been driven in somewhere, somehow, and conflict resulted. Bingo! Communication has broken down. We've learned that if you can find and deal with the issue causing separation—the germs, by analogy—the conflict, the symptom, takes care of itself.

When that cannot be done, you must treat the symptom. And when this happens, usually the cause—the germ—emerges and you can treat it.

"Aha!" you say. "So if I let 'er rip and encourage conflict, my marriage will grow stronger. Good! I love to argue."

That's not what we're saying at all! We're saying that you can turn the friction inevitable in any honest union into an asset. Food is a good illustration. We must have it; eat or die. And yet, used wrongly, food becomes the center of all sorts of problems, from anorexia to malnutrition to obesity.

To make conflict productive, you must stick to the rules.

"There are rules?" you ask.

Of course. You know there are *always* rules.

Rules of Conflict Resolution

Rules of conflict resolution don't work during conflicts. In the heat of disagreement, when your very self is on the line, you don't think of following rules. And, if you do think of it, you don't want to anyway, lest by following the rules you lose. There are, however, some guidelines to prevent the buildup of hostility that squashes intimacy in your relationship. You can explore these guidelines *before* another damaging conflict arises in your marriage. Then you'll be prepared the next time.

There are things to consider before the next storm breaks, things to remember during the actual conflict, and things to reflect upon afterwards. All can help you understand and speak to your mate. And that is intimacy.

For example, let's guide Rick and Nancy through some healthy changes in conflict management and intimacy.

Things to Ponder Before *the Storm*

1. Know Yourself

First, understand and be aware of what's going on inside yourself. Explore your family-of-origin issues. How about codependent tendencies? What's making you tick, deep inside?

Think how you felt during prior fights (Not what was said, but how you felt).

Now, think why you may have felt this way. Was there anything in your past that may have snuck into the argument?

Nancy, for example, was an adult child of divorce. Her parents, both professional people, separated when she was seventeen, filing the papers a week after her high school graduation. Guess what. Nancy's youngest child graduated just a few days before one of her and Rick's biggest blow-ups. And Nancy and Rick have never really been at peace since. And as Nancy thought about it more, another big super-argument had occurred about the time of their elder son's graduation.

Nancy had a time bomb at the bottom of her mind. That bomb whispered, "It's time to part. Repeat the pattern of your parents and separate now. Based on your own past, you know it's divorce time." Conflict, so to speak, played right into the hands of that sinister time-release capsule.

In counseling we often suggest that chronic warriors fold a piece of paper in half vertically. On the left, they are to write down all the commonly-heard phrases in a recent argument, not necessarily in order. We ask them to write on the right side of the paper the corresponding feelings they had, and still have, for each statement.

Some of Nancy's feelings were:

"I feel angry. I'm the only one who cares about this marriage."

"I feel like I'm being taken advantage of."

"I can't stand the way he refuses to change his mind. He says he'll change or he'll do this or that, and a week later, nothing's changed."

How do the statements made during the heat of an argument agree with the feelings behind them? Often, in this stage, they don't match up much at all. The spouses feel fury, specific resentments, bitterness, hurt, fear, and hopelessness. But they don't say those things. Instead, they say the same blame words or put-downs they've been speaking for fifteen years.

Until Nancy explores what her true feelings are, and some of the reasons for them, she won't be able to express them. She won't get past that non-communication barrier.

2. Think

Have you ever analyzed a television series episode? Try it sometime. You'll find an unvarying pattern. For instance, the one-hour adventure show: In the first two minutes, a lot of attention-getting things happen to "hook" you into staying on that channel. The plot thickens in a hurry. The first commercial break happens at an odd moment. The second commercial break occurs on the half-hour (every time). Because this is when channel-changers are most likely to hop around, the hero will be in the utmost danger, the situation at a frightening nadir. You can't change channels now. Character development, if any, occurs before the third commercial break. During the final segment, the villain appears to win. Then the plot does a flipflop and the hero comes out on top. The series usually concludes with a wrap-up.

Millions of Americans are exposed to this unvarying pattern of entertainment every night. Television, by rote formula, does all the thinking for us. Some shows even do the philosophizing for us in the wrap-up, eliminating any need to think at all. Yet, unless people are trained to think, and are practiced in considering options, they can't resolve conflicts.

Anyone surviving a high school debating class knows that you must be able to debate either side of an argument if you're to present your position effectively. You must know the other side's strengths and weaknesses.

And so we ask persons in counseling to reflect on their spouse's side of the argument in some recent conflict, using the same folded-paper technique.

Nancy wrote Rick's comments on the left.

"It doesn't matter."

"Look, you're making a big deal out of something that's a nickel-and-dime thing."

And when he really got mad at her for pressing a point, "Will you just chill out?"

We would then ask Nancy to write what she thought Rick's feelings behind his statements might be. That was something she would have to really think about. She would have to consider his past and his present, perhaps even the possibilities for his future as he sees them.

"Rick has been in essentially the same dead-end job for the last seven years. I can see where he'd feel some bitterness, maybe even losing hope for advancement."

"My career is doing well. Could he feel threatened? Maybe even jealous or resentful?"

Were Nancy to examine Rick's standard comebacks and phrases in their arguments, she would see and hear an undercurrent of hopelessness ("It doesn't matter"). She could see where he would feel threatened when she pushed and she would begin to recognize, behind his thick shell of resistance, a frightened, hurting "little boy" who did not know how to please his parents as a child and who did not know how to communicate his feelings to his wife.

Rick's real posture in their conflict was, in fact, "I feel like a midlife failure. I'm afraid you'll think less of me if I share this fear and make myself vulnerable to you. So, instead, I'll keep my feelings bottled up and seal them off with a layer of anger."

Now try this exercise yourself. Using two folded papers, write your statements and your spouse's, focus on a recent conflict. Write what fears and positions you think might be lurking underneath these statements. Now try to summarize those feelings in both you and your spouse.

Write what your position is:

_____

_____

_____

Write what you think your spouse's position is:

_____

_____

_____

The next time conflict erupts, you will have some insight into what is really happening, down below the words.

Things That Will Help During the Storm

1. Avoid Absolutes

It's natural for arguing couples to throw missiles back and forth at each other. If both parties know themselves and are thinking, however, they can call a cease-fire to the accusations. This is much easier if you _never_ speak in absolutes:

- "You're _always_ working late."
- "You _never_ plan ahead."
- "You _never_ help around the house."
- "You've _never_ really loved me."

Absolute statements usually guarantee a hot retort back because they're overstated. Even if they're true ninety-nine percent of the time, the spouse will be quick to come back with that other one percent.

Nancy caught herself saying "You never care!" during every argument.

2. Avoid "You" Statements

Character assassinations or criticism do not resolve conflicts.

- "You're so selfish, all you think about is yourself."
- "You're getting to be just like your father." How would you feel if someone were saying these things to you? Ready to capitulate?

That's not what you really want to say, anyway.

For "you" statements, try to substitute "I" statements.

- "I feel lonely around you much of the time. When you withdraw from me into self-preoccupation, I blame myself and I fear you don't really love me."
- "I'm afraid you're picking up some of your father's bad habits, and it scares me. I fear I'll be treated as your mother was."

3. Stick to the Basics

Nancy's arguments always ended up in diatribes about Rick's lackadaisical attitudes and predictability, whether that was part of the opening salvo or not. If the argument is about who left the cap off the toothpaste, keep it there.

Nancy snorted. "If we only argued about the subject, when would I tell him what I think of him?"

And we might suggest, "How about telling some positive, supportive thoughts you have about him, at bedtime?"

In the heat of battle, that is much easier said than done. It helps if you . . .

4. Keep the People Out of the Fight

Huh?

Sure, it's the people having the fight. But issues and persons are two different entities. Argue over the issues, but never allow arguments to get personal. Keep emotions at bay. When the need to win a disagreement becomes overpowering, it will control your emotions and your tongue. You end up in a brutal dogfight. Dogs fight each other, not issues.

Love and intimacy become the first victims of your battle.

Brian Newman says: "We see it constantly in couples we counsel. Once a conflict becomes emotional, reason goes out the door and the conflict will never be resolved. We help the couple keep it from becoming personal, by any of several ways. One way is to ask them to be creative."

Part of being creative about conflict is being able to see options clearly. A good option is simply to back off and cool off.

Debi Newman explains, "So very often we talk to Christian couples. They quote us the passage, 'Be angry, but do not sin; do not let the sun go down on your anger.' The man and woman interpret this to mean that their anger has to be resolved quickly, before they go to sleep. So they take that anger to bed with them and hash it over then. Lights out may be the first time the couple is alone together and can talk about it.

"Or, in order to get rid of the anger, they end up denying it, and burying it deep within the recesses of their subconscious.

"We try to get them to see that dealing with anger does not always mean getting rid of it or resolving it right away. It's simply not always possible. By all means, address that anger before the 'sun goes down.' But you might have to address it by agreeing not to deal with it now; you'll deal with it later. Then set a definite time later to do that. You might not sleep any better, but you will get cooling-off time."

Frank Minirth agrees, "Don't lie in bed, tired and frustrated, and expect to hash out the issue. You don't have the ability to look at options then, to think rationally. You're tired and want to go to sleep. To be creative in dealing with conflict, you must be fresh enough to think."

We all need breathing space—time out. Most people need to dispel the physical rush associated with anger and frustration. Throw rocks into a pond, run a mile, beat a rug, anything to sap the adrenaline rush that anger gave you. Indeed, you might have to postpone your discussion more than once if the fire isn't banked.

Cooling-off time is not wasted time. There are many ways you can use this time constructively. Write your spouse a letter, pouring out every last ounce of fury. Then burn it. Just getting your thoughts down on paper will help your rational thought patterns and better prepare you for the confrontation when it happens.

You can also get creative in ways to defuse the anger. One couple in our counsel hit upon a diversion by accident. In their early years of marriage, the wife would exclaim in the middle of the heated argument, "All I know how to do is love!" Years later, they both use this line during a disagreement and end up giggling. Situation defused.

Nancy and Rick, on the other hand, didn't want to defuse the situation. Down deep, they *wanted* to fight. You see, fights were the only times they really faced each other and said things, even if the things they said were old, stale, and predictable. They were going to have to go against their hidden need to fight and beat it down. One way to do that would be to find face-to-face time in a non-combative situation.

They'd almost forgotten how.

After the Storm

Resolution

Fights are not resolved by fighting. You're a veteran of enough spats to know that. Rick and Nancy's set-tos never ended satisfactorily. They dissolved in his shouts or her tears. Eventually one or the other would refuse to say another word. The silence would last a couple of days. A few words, a few requests to pass the salt, and the fire would subside.

The fire was never put out. It was banked until the next time. Although Rick and Nancy—and you—cannot always expect immediate resolution to conflicts, you and they must always look toward some sort of eventual resolution. That resolution will take one of three forms: compromise, an agreement to disagree, or a love gift.

Compromise

One side gives, the other gives, the problem is solved. That's what Frank and Mary Alice Minirth decided to do when they purchased vacation property. A friend of theirs tells about the compromise: "Frank is a country boy. He likes animals, he likes rural living. Mary Alice is a city girl. They have a place in rural Arkansas—I mean, *very* rural. Cabins, horses, undeveloped land. As you approach their property, you see no power poles, no hints of modern conveniences at all. It looks the same as it did a hundred and fifty years ago. But inside the cabins are up-to-date kitchen appliances, dishwashers and microwaves. The outside of the property is Frank's concept of country living; the inside is Mary Alice's. It's a lovely compromise and works beautifully for both of them."

Compromise takes real communication.

1. Actively listen. Hear your partner's words with your ears, and listen for some place where you can give a little. Identify the places where you're not going to give an inch for love or money.

2. *Now say those thoughts out loud.* "I can't budge on this part of it. I will, though, give you this other part."

As both partners actively listen for what is said, for what is not said, for chinks where compromise can gain a foothold, intimacy improves. You're getting to know the real person better.

Agreement to Disagree

During counseling, couples often express surprise that agreeing to disagree is an option. Why not? Some black-and-white issues cannot be resolved to grey. Intimacy does not mean agreeing on every issue. It means knowing where your partner stands and being able to live with that. Knowing where your partner stands comes only by talking to each other, truly talking to each other.

Debi Newman explains, "For example, when one spouse is very controlling, it's important that the other not constantly cave in just to avoid conflict. That's an open door to unhealthy polarization. Polarization is when people move to opposite ends of a seesaw, whatever the seesaw may be (he sleeps in, she gets up early; he makes the decisions, she backs out of decision-making). The controlling spouse becomes all the more controlling, and the other begins to lose identity and self-esteem. The situation—giving in, I mean—certainly generates anger, and that's not good for either the spouses or the marriage."

Rick insists that the kids should be able to consider the car home, and eat popcorn in the back seat, chew gum, make themselves comfortable. Nancy insists that the last thing their car upholstery needs is chewing gum and greasy popcorn (and the cheese that drips from a cheeseburger . . . and . . . the list goes on). They could not arrange a sensible compromise (the kids eating only on the return trip, for example, is not sensible).

Rick's position, which he would express in carefully chosen words (that is, not heated words): "I know it annoys you to have to vacuum the car, and I know you don't want the kids eating back there, but I do. And I'm going to let them."

Nancy's position, which she would articulate in a non-threatening atmosphere: "I am still adamantly opposed. The kids can eat before and after. They don't need snacks during. I'll keep looking for a win-win compromise, but don't bet we'll find one."

Their positions are stated. Each understands the other's. It is not the most satisfactory of resolutions, but it serves. The argument is ended.

Love Gift

Some would call it "giving in." If that is what it is in fact, the resolution is lost. Were Nancy to allow a love gift to resolve an argument, she would take the attitude, "This means a lot to Rick. I have a valid point, but he's not going to budge. For the sake of resolution, I'll give it to him." And she would probably add, "And he better understand that I'm doing it out of love and not just to restore peace."

Obviously a love gift has to be given without anger or resentment or it won't be a healthy response. And both sides must understand that it is an act of love.

Lou and Marj Ajanian's neighbors, Bert and Meg, illustrate this. Lou and Bert sat on Bert's front porch one afternoon reflecting on marriage.

"Meg's been a proper wife these past forty-three years. Submissive. What I say goes." Bert said. "How about your Marj?"

Lou pondered that. "Well first of all. Marj isn't 'my' anything. She's always been her own woman. Never afraid to speak her mind. And, she keeps me out of plenty of scrapes with her wisdom." Lou sat quietly awhile, thinking about his first wife, now deceased. She was no shrinking violet, either. He remembered the steadfast love she had given him over their years together, and tears filled his eyes.

Meg gave into Bert every time. Eventually she became the "doormat" to his feet. Did Bert love her? He claimed he did and he probably did in his way. Did Meg love Bert? Perhaps. In response to Bert's domineering attitude, she found it easier and easier to give in as time went by. Angry at first that she had no effective voice in this marriage, she resigned herself to the situation. That anger numbed out, becoming depression. She lived a life free of conflict, but at a terrible price. She would eventually die a very miserable woman.

In this case, the love gift became, with time, a painful cop-out. Neither love nor a gift.

None of these methods of resolution is appropriate to every situation. Be aware of becoming locked into one approach at the exclusion of the others, as Bert and Meg did. You and your spouse should be using the full range of resolutions of conflict. Your goal is to establish new patterns of speaking to each other.

Rick and Nancy used fights for communication. For awhile, conflict was the only communication between them, and not very good communication at that. Rick and Nancy established new patterns by using conflict-resolution skills. They at last could talk to each other without raising voices and without opposing each other. They had ceased taking each other for granted.

Nancy could still predict what Rick would say in casual social situations, but she no longer so glibly predicted his responses to arguments. They had changed.

If you've figured out how to use conflict to improve your intimacy, how then can you build on that intimacy to further improve your marriage?

Build Intimacy

How might one build true intimacy, as opposed to the stifling closeness of a codependent relationship? "Miracles happen when you learn to date again," says Frank Minirth. "To improve intimacy, start dating. Take walks together, exercise together. They build intimacy."

Mary Alice relates, "Frank and I pray together, but it's not an organized thing. He'll hold my hand and say, 'Let's pray.' We prayed together over the phone from the hospital, when he was worried about Dad."

Frank offers this caveat, however. "We don't overly analyze everything in our marriage. We just enjoy each other. If we always knew everything going on in each other's head, we'd always have conflict and we couldn't get through the passages. Too much or not enough [introspection] are both damaging.

"The final note is, the idealism never left our relationship. We never lost it. You don't need to lose your idealism. If you have, you can restore it by what you do and how you think. We restructure our thinking and behavior. Behavior controls feelings."

Frank ends with a point few people like to think about, but it's important. "Don't be so dependent that you don't have your own identity. You're going to have to say good-bye sometime, and then you'll have to be a whole person, able to enjoy life."

"There is such a thing as good denial," Frank Minirth explains. "If we realized too quickly everything negative about ourselves and our marriage, our lives and the passages, we'd all decompensate. We have to work through our problems over time. What I call 'good denial' lines up the ducks instead of a duck attack all at once. Bad denial prevents us from seeing what we should see, what we must see. Without some denial, though, we'd be overloaded—more than we can handle. Good denial is not a deliberate thing, but it works. Denial becomes pathological when it keeps us from progressing and growing; when it promotes conflict."

Mary Alice explains good denial. "My dad fought cancer many years. Two days after chemotherapy treatments he was home working, mowing the yard. He was still working at a job, fifteen years after diagnosis. He was a building superintendent. He worked with cancer until he retired at 63. He died at 71. Keeping going contributed to his success. There is something to say for denial. Life has all kinds of reality and circumstance; you can let it pull you under, or use a little healthy denial and just keep going, ignoring the poor odds."

In addition to good denial, idealism, and romanticism, flexibility also helps build intimacy in all relationships, not just marriages. The world today would be a lot better off if everyone practiced some form of tolerance and flexibility.

Flexibility

It is absolutely critical, if one is to smooth out the speed bumps in the road to marital harmony, to be flexible when meeting life. This required flexibility exists in several dimensions.

For one, couples must be open to major changes in each other. For example, there was Earl Jr., up in Maine. His whole life, Earl's father worked in a factory. It wasn't what Earl Sr. enjoyed—he had always wanted to run a gas station or auto repair shop. But assembly line work paid well enough, and when the factory whistle blew, Earl's dad could turn his back on work, go home, and veg out with TV.

Earl Jr. slipped easily into that comfortable rut too. He didn't enjoy factory work any more than his dad did, but, as Earl Sr. said, it paid well enough. Earl Jr., though, didn't stay in the rut. He had always yearned to be a lobsterman. As he looked back on the first thirty-five years of his life, taking stock, he decided that if he was ever going realize that dream he must do it now. Instead of going home to TV, he leased an old lobster boat and put forty pots out. Hauling traps in all weather was no easy work, but Earl Jr. made enough in five years to buy his own boat and quit the factory.

That first summer his wife had a conniption. But she mellowed to the idea, especially when she realized how much happier Earl was. They talked about it and shared dreams. By the time Earl served notice at the factory, she was with him one hundred percent—well, ninety-five, at least.

Earl's wife's dreams had never included lobsters. Knowing how marginal shellfishing is as an occupation, she feared greatly for their future. She had to make major adjustments, difficult adjustments, to cope with her fear and adapt to Earl's dream.

Look, though, at the beautiful lines of communication Earl and his wife maintained. They talked. They made sure each knew where the other stood. They bent when bending was necessary, they hung in when obstinateness served best. Communication at its best.

Mary Alice Minirth sums it up well. "Flexibility, fighting fear, and faith. Three F's. For better or worse, all our ways are colored by them. Faith in God's plan enhances faith in each other and commitment. Faith in each other helps you roll with the punches and be flexible. It helps you master fear. And it helps you stay with the fundamentals of life, the important things.

"My dad coped with cancer a long time. If he had feared cancer and let that fear control him, he wouldn't have lived another nineteen years. When I couldn't have babies, and kept trying: if I didn't have faith in God's plan, I would have given up. We almost did. I came so close to letting fear envelop me. Some people are better at mastering fear than others, but all can work at it. When you get past fear, God blesses your life with fruitfulness, and you have faith in your future."

How specifically does one develop flexibility? Mary Alice grins. "Frank says we'd be bored if we were normal. No one is 'normal,'" and she makes quotation marks in the air with her fingers. "The trick to flexibility is, you have to just accept circumstances—you're never going to be normal, nobody is. We're all unique. When life circumstances change, or make your spouse respond in a new way, step back and think; can I give on this?

Flex on this? What shall I do so I don't become fearful or para-
noid and turn this Third Passage into a disaster?"

Mary Alice herself provides an excellent example of flexing
with the circumstances. Again, the situation began by taking
stock. "Four years ago I was always screaming at the kids to get
in the car to go to lessons or something all the time. When I
realized what was happening, I flat out quit it for two years.

"It was tough. My daughter Renee said, 'Mom, I really
wanted ballet this year.' And I said, 'We have barnyard this year.'
All the kids had to do for fun was mess around on the farm.
Then we started to pick things up now and then, but not like it
used to be.

"The kids still spend lots of time down at the barn. School is
high key, goal-oriented. The kids go down to the barn after
school. They're so tense when they get home, and all laid-back
when they return from the barn. The kids are always grooming,
picking hooves, and working with the horses. Their messing-
around time is a release."

The Minirth children had to be flexible to shift from the hectic
pace to the leisurely one, but Mary Alice recalls having to make
some major adjustments herself.

"I'm not a farm or animal-oriented person at all. The Lord
showed me how good it is for the kids and Frank, so I've bought
into the program. There was this time, I just had a manicure and
then I had to hoofpick the horse . . ." She smiles. "I've come a
long way. I didn't dream of that as my role in life. Ever. But I see
how healthy it is for my husband and kids . . ." and she shrugs.

Flexibility seems easy enough to establish. But what if your
problems seem far too large to merely give in and relax your
standards on? What if you've come to the point of an ultimatum?

Chapter 4

The Now-or-Never Syndrome

*I*lona Guthrie couldn't remember exactly. Perhaps it was the day Reede forgot to fasten the tailgate when he was hauling the kids' 4-H sheep in the pick-up truck, and all nine ewes jumped out and ran through Mrs. Ware's flower beds; and then Mrs. Ware's dog chased after them clear around her house, and on the second time around they ran over Mrs. Ware. Or maybe it was the time Reede installed the drip irrigation system in the front yard himself, instead of hiring professionals, and they turned it on but nothing happened, and two hours later they got this frantic call from Harry next door that the flood in his basement was a foot deep and rising. No matter. Whatever the exact occasion, there was a day, a moment, when Ilona fell out of love with Reede.

The Guthries, married fifteen years, had three children between the ages of five and twelve, the two boys and the kindergarten-aged girl. The oldest, Wayne, was a good kid, but too smart. He was in all these sports and clubs after school, and Ilona spent half her day in the car fetching him to and from it all. Jeffrey, the next son, would end up in jail if Ilona didn't kill him first. Boy, that kid could pull some lulus!

Little Marcy, though. There was Ilona's saving grace, her little daughter. Marcy was so cute, and very mature for her age. Ilona could depend on Marcy to tell her if the boys were getting into something bad, and Marcy always brought Ilona a smile, usually when she needed one most, and Marcy would never be the do-nothing Reede turned out to be.

Ilona had thought of divorce. She felt it was either "now-or-never." After all she was thirty-three, and she wasn't sure she'd have much of a chance to remarry if she didn't do something *now*. Still, the kids needed a family to be in, and what would she gain by a divorce? Reede would still be Reede, an irritating pain in the posterior, whether she was with him or not, and he was, after all, the children's father. Besides, he managed to hold down a job, though not a prestigious one, and it paid pretty well since he got in-service pay increases. Shucks, he'd been doing the same job their whole marriage: driving a truck. No promotions, no managing something, just driving. Hmmph.

The Guthries farmed on the side, mostly so the kids could have their pony and their 4-H projects. Four-H made a big impact on them.

On Mrs. Ware too.

Disenchanted

When Ilona Guthrie first married Reede she was as much in love as any eighteen-year-old, and more than most. Of course, at twenty she didn't see all the flaws that, through time, forced disenchantment upon her. Ilona did not consider marriage counseling because Reede was the problem, and he would never change. That was just the way Reede was.

Ilona illustrates perfectly the malaise into which a marriage can sink during this Third Passage. Fortunately, Ilona also illustrates how you can turn a faded marriage around, for she did just that. The third task of this passage is to overcome the now-or-never syndrome, the disillusionment that is frequent during this passage and is compounded by the fear, "It's now or never. I've got to turn this marriage around or get out of this marriage so I can build another life."

The Third Task: To Overcome the Now-or-Never
Syndrome

Considerable temptation looms in this Third Passage. Temptations to quit trying and just get a divorce; to seek with someone else what you feel is lacking in your marriage (understanding, affection, whatever); to marry your job, because on the job you get all sorts of positive strokes and at home you get nagged.

If you've been married ten years or longer, weigh your marriage as you consider these points. If you've been married less than ten years, these points may give you insight into the future. Wouldn't it be lovely to be prepared for disillusionment? Forewarned is forearmed.

Ilona overcame the now-or-never syndrome by learning to accept the losses that she saw in her marriage, many of which were inevitable in any marriage.

The Illusion of a Perfect Mate

Think, for the moment, upon your mate: irritations, good points, lousy habits, shortfalls, strong points.

Debi Newman explains the importance of keeping a balance as you perform this first part of taking stock. "As you think about your mate, get your anger and discontent out in the open where you can see it. We often ask our patients to write out the negative aspects of their mate's personality."

We suggest that you name three right now:
(For example, "My spouse is always much more quick to criticize me than to praise me.")

1. _____
2. _____
3. _____

What on this list *really* pushes your buttons? What disturbs you most? Frequently what seems to be a very disturbing factor to one spouse may actually be a mirror of some sort of unresolved pain in his or her family-of-origin. It's not that the factor isn't there. It usually is. But the spouse is overreacting to it. Might that be the case with any of the aspects you've listed above? How might one or more of them mirror problems in your childhood family? What are situations or memories from your family of origin that may make you overly sensitive to certain traits in your spouse?

(For example, "My father was highly critical of me and that fact makes me extremely sensitive to criticism from my spouse.")

1. _____

2. _____

3. _____

We treated one couple, Bernie and Beverly Engle, in which the wife was deeply concerned about her husband's ability to manage money. It had not been an issue during their first two passages; there had not been enough money to manage as they were starting out. Now, in their Third Passage, they were beginning to plan for their future, to look closely at the mortgage, to consider the kids' college funds, and their own retirement. Beverly's concerns escalated.

Actually, Bernie was not too bad. Though no wizard, he did all right with their conservative investments. But that wasn't good enough for her. As Beverly explored her family-of-origin, she discovered that her grandfather had lost a sizable family fortune in the Depression. That wound, untreated, had been handed down through her father to her. As she grieved it, and discussed it with her parents, the excessive demands she made on her husband to be the perfect financial manager moderated.

Expectations are not the only factors. Obviously you can't have a strong marriage if you don't respect your spouse. Ilona had a hard, hard time coming to grips with Reede's weaknesses, just as all couples do. We even admit to having that problem ourselves.

"Frank is obsessively goal-oriented—he's a workaholic, but he's not super-organized in some other ways," says Mary Alice Minirth. "Strong points and weak points. I did pray a long time ago that I wouldn't marry someone who just comes home and reads the paper. I'd much rather be married to him than a lazy person. He cares. He cares deeply, which is a common characteristic of workaholics."

Think about what Mary Alice said. She found the secret: She appreciates that the weaknesses are related to the strengths, and therefore both strengths and weaknesses together contribute to the excellent man he is. Not just the strengths—the weaknesses as well.

Ilona looked at Reede's strengths, and she didn't mind admitting she had to really dig to root them out. He was steady; the same job all those years, faithful to her from the start. He never once changed a diaper, all three kids, but he was always there to help them with their pony, or their 4-H projects. He was just as free with his time helping their friends at their behest, and the local 4-H chapter depended upon him heavily, for many of the kids' parents didn't have the time, let alone a pick-up truck.

Now bring out in the open all the positive things about your spouse also:

(For example, "My spouse sets high standards for himself, and I admire his values.")

1._____
2._____
3._____

We call these two exercises a positive-negative appraisal. Strangely, the better you are able to be honest about your spouse's flaws and grieve them, the better able you will be to enjoy your spouse's positive qualities. That's why we ask our patients to clarify the positives and negatives.

Now what do you actually do with these lists you've written and insights you've made? We suggest several things.

One constructive use is to make the lists the basis for mutual improvement in weak areas. Sit down together, never in the heat of anger or debate but during some peaceful time, and open negotiations. Beverly Engle tackled the issue while she and her husband relaxed by their fireplace late one night.

First, explain to your spouse what you see as some major deficiencies of your own. Not only are you opening dialogue, you're opening it in a nonthreatening and nonblaming way. You're discussing deficiencies in general and owning your own weaknesses.

Next, identify the realistic areas of concern you have about your spouse's attitudes, positions, or performance. Don't dump the whole list on the poor person at once. One topic is sufficient at a time. In Beverly's case, it would be her concern about their long-range financial picture and who would paint it.

Third, having thought it out thoroughly beforehand, acknowledge your own contribution to the degree of your concern. In this woman's case, her family's old, unspoken, long-standing fears about financial safety colored her own attitude.

Fourth, ask for constructive changes in your spouse. No demands, no whining, no hostility, no threats. The spouse is free to grant the request or not. Beverly asked that the two of them review the financial records quarterly. Bernie then would either agree, refuse, or modify the request. How about once a year instead? Bernie queried.

Fifth, and this is the most important step, both parties affirm the positive qualities they see in each other. This is the list of positives you made. "Don't be so fed up with negatives," Debi Newman warns, "that you fail to bring out the good qualities of your spouse." For instance, Beverly Engle expressed her appreciation that her man, whether financial whiz or not, was a constant and loving mate, dependable, possessing strong spiritual roots.

Regardless the outcome of your session, employ one sixth and final step. Use humor and grief to make peace with reality, particularly with chronic stuck areas that don't seem to change. The wife must grieve the scars her family carried for three generations. They will always be there to some degree. Probably, Bernie will never be quite the financial whiz she'd prefer. Humor will salve the hurt. It will help her deal with the realization that life isn't perfect.

There are other ways, too, to utilize these lists. One way is to use your spouse's strengths to deal with his/her weaknesses more effectively. For example, clients of ours, Bill and Candace Johnson. Candace had a different problem from Beverly Engle's. Candace was married to Bill—a man who was certain he was the financial whiz of the family. Bill didn't listen to anything Candace had to say. His less-than-illustrious investment record told Candace maybe he ought to listen to her. Bill Johnson's big strength was that he could read vast amounts of material quickly and extract the meat of the information. So rather than encourage Bill to set up such-and-so retirement account, Candace would circle articles in finance journals. As long as Bill was reading it in print, he was open to its message. Were Candace to give him the same information from her own lips, he would have disregarded it. Candace thus used Bill's strengths to slip past his weaknesses.

If your mate responds better to written words than spoken words, leave notes around the house, or in your spouse's brief-case, or taped to the steering wheel. If your spouse is a cracker-jack accountant who can't remember appointments worth beans, provide an appointment calendar built like a ledger sheet. What on that list of positive attributes can you work with to help com-bat the negative attributes?

Susan Hemfelt recalls how she was able to overcome her irrita-tion with one of Robert's annoying habits by focusing on a posi-tive attribute. "Robert leaves about a billion partially-empty shampoo bottles all over the place." She explained, "I'm totally different. I use up one bottle, throw it in the recycle bin, and open another. His habit used to drive me right up the wall.

"Then I noticed how he was the only one of us who could shampoo the kids' hair without getting any soap in their eyes, ever! When I washed their hair, I always got some soap in their eyes—which the kids would remind me of whenever it was my turn for their baths ('Oh no, not Mom'). I even thought about buying one of those rubber headbands they can wear which pro-tects their face from dripping soap suds.

"When I watched Robert wash their hair, I noticed it was much easier for him to keep the soap out of the eyes of a squirm-ing kid while using one of those partially-empty shampoo bottles than it was for me. Now, I can tolerate the litter of shampoo bottles in the bathroom. I even tell the kids how much better their Dad is at washing their hair than I am."

This is a case where a negative attribute was overcome by the effectiveness of a positive trait in the eyes of the beholder. But what about when a negative trait can be overwhelming?

Another way to use the positive-negative appraisal is to moni-tor those kind of weaknesses (negative attributes). Too often, they become addictive or codependent behaviors. The whole family system, then, begins to rotate around that behavior, al-lowing for it, catering to it, avoiding it, working around it. The classic case is the alcohol dependency of one family member around which all the rest of the family tiptoe. Look down the list again. Any chance those weaknesses can escalate into something that hurts the family system?

Last, and most important of all, we urge that you, as we do constantly, give thanks for the positive traits you see for you and for your spouse. Then grieve through and forgive the negative aspects you recognize in yourself and the negative aspects you have confronted in your spouse.

The Grieving Process

For those of you unfamiliar with the grieving process, we will review it here. The grieving process was first defined and oulined by Elizabeth Kubler-Ross and was also discussed in *Love Is a Choice* (Nashville: Thomas Nelson, 1989). For those of you familiar with it, consider the following discussion as a brief review.

The first step in the grieving process is *shock and denial.* It is a natural step. You may be shocked at a negative trait your spouse has pointed out and you will probably deny its existence.

The next step involves *depression.* Again this emotion is natural. Expect depression in any grieving situation. If depression becomes exceedingly severe or lingers too long (months and months, for example), we suggest you seek medical help.

The third step, *bargaining,* is usually unrecognized by the grieving person, but it happens. Bargaining and magical thinking are part of grieving and should be temporary. Bargaining is an effort to skirt around the grief issue rather than face it directly. "If I make more money will that make you happy?" you might say when your spouse's irritation with your negative traits is on your spending sprees. That bargaining will not take care of the negative trait, however. Guard, though, against letting one of your bargains or magical thoughts turn into a plan of action. Magic won't help you. Alcoholics are particularly adept at bargaining, and they make it their plan of action.

The next step is *sadness.* You may feel genuinely sad when you come to accept one of your not-so-good attributes. That's good, you're on the way to resolving your grief. It's natural and very necessary to feel sad when grieving, let no one tell you otherwise.

The final phase of grieving is *forgiveness and resolution.* They bring a measure of peace, but they do not close the book or ease the pain. The person you need to forgive if you are dealing with grieving a negative attribute of yourself is yourself. Resolution is the healthy outcome of any grieving process. You and your spouse might want to come up with a workable method to help each other overcome his/her negative attributes.

You won't ever be finished with the grieving process. It will come up time and time again throughout your life. Repeatedly at different stages of marriage, it will be necessary to grieve the multiple ways in which your spouse does not live up to the ideal picture of a mate. We will refer to the grieving process several times in this book alone. Only by using the steps we mentioned above, will you be able to work through the grief. You cannot shortcut any of the steps, you must pass through all of them. You might get sandtrapped into one step for a long period of time, but only by going through all the steps in order, will you resolve your loss.

"Grief is not a one-and-done action," explains Robert Hemfelt. "We have to grieve both the awareness of the negative trait in ourselves and the damage that trait has inflicted on other relationships in the family. So sometimes we have to go back and grieve through something again and again. The actual importance of a loss has nothing to do with it, either. It's the relative importance, the importance of that loss to you personally, that determines how much healthful grieving will occur. One person may lose a beloved five-thousand-dollar purebred show dog and his neighbor loses a beloved pound mutt. Both losses are extremely heavy. The key is 'beloved,' not monetary value."

One of the big blahs of the Third Passage exists in the bedroom. The bedroom, as you know, mirrors the living room. Spiffing one up helps the other, and when one gets dull the other does too. Ilona Guthrie had to grieve the losses in her sexual relationship with Reede.

The Illusion of Perfect Sex and Romance

"My sex life?" Ilona smirked. "It was a big yawn, a yawn of boredom and a yawn of pure exhaustion."

By the Third Passage, sexual partners are usually pretty well settled into a deep rut of routines and patterns.

Even unpredictability can be predictable. In our counseling

with a woman with other problems, we learned that every couple of years her husband threatened to quit his job, put everything behind him, and go to Australia and raise sheep. The first time or two she found his threats very frightening. Eventually, she could see it coming. She came to know it was just his way of blowing off steam. He wasn't *really* going to pack the whole family off to the outback.

Like that woman, we all come to know our mates' daily, monthly, multi-yearly cycles. The routine permeates all the other areas of our lives and spills into the bedroom.

A goal of this Third Passage, then, is to combat apathy. We encourage weekly dates to get away from the house and kids. This can be a time for the couple to take retreats—marriage enrichment weekends or a cruise together. Get a family member to stay with the kids for a week. Rekindle and make fresh the sensuality in your marriage.

A comfort/discomfort paradox exists here too. It's responsible in large part for the middle-age crazies you sometimes see. Emotionally and perhaps hormonally, love has wound down somewhat. The husband and wife have settled in comfortably enough. That is, they're established, and that comfort gives them the time to examine their discomforts. People in the First and Second Passages gloss over the discomforts as they try to carve out an identity as a couple and start the family, get the career rolling, and bond together. Those are enormous distractors, leaving scant time and energy to focus on: "Is this the ultimate dream of my heart?" They match their romantic fantasy against reality and find reality sadly discomforting.

The problem multiplies when it appears that other people in other couplings appear to be living out their fantasies. "They're getting it all and I'm cheated."

Dreams are lovely. They're wonderful human drivers. But they must be balanced with the reality. No human being can provide the ultimate romantic union. This is the passage when couples finally get around to making peace with the disparity between fantasy and reality, the dream and the day-to-day.

What do you do about it? Hold onto the dreams as a goal toward which to work. At the same time, grieve to the point of acceptance the fact that you won't meet your dreams perfectly. Avoid the even more dangerous illusion that if your spouse will never complete your fantasy someone else might. It is just that, an illusion. This type of thinking gets you stuck back in that First Passage, and the New Love passage is by no means the most satisfying and enriching period your marriage can enjoy.

Sensuality takes a beating in this passage, too, and must be grieved like any other loss. Major time and energy distractions, from the kids, schedules, and careers, put sex on a back burner— or take it off the stove altogether.

"Doctor, it feels like just pure survival. We're so harried, we collapse in bed exhausted, get up the next morning, and start it all over." Over and over, we hear that in counsel and among our friends. For them, at best, sex becomes a hurried release of sexual urges. At worst, the couples here begin long periods of sexual abstinence because of sheer exhaustion.

How much time do you and your spouse spend *each week* in sexually oriented intimacy (that is, not the intimacy of talking together at breakfast—only that intimacy which surrounds the sexual union)? Can that time be measured with:

_____ a stopwatch?
_____ the bedroom alarm clock?
_____ a calendar?

Once you have made peace with these losses, you can turn your energies to building a better marriage during this Third Passage. By the way, as the marriage is revitalized in a general sense through grieving the loss of the ideal and commiting to new growth, you may be in for some pleasant surprises in the bedroom. One way will be to build up your spouse. You've been working on a new you. Now you can take definite steps to provide your new you with a new mate.

Build up Your Spouse

Robert Hemfelt and Brian and Debi Newman were discussing one afternoon the ways marital partners can build each other up and improve their self-esteem. "Encouragement is vital, important and necessary," Robert Hemfelt began.

"Absolutely!" Brian Newman nodded vigorously. "It sounds so obvious. But if you grow up in a family where people don't encourage one another spontaneously, you may be oblivious to how important it is. It's just as important or more so than sunshine, oxygen, and nutrition."

"Some people think it's selfish," Debi Newman added. "It's not at all selfish to want it. Encouragement is a basic need in life."

"What most people fail to see," Robert continued, "is that discouragement is terribly toxic."

"Terribly." Brian tapped a psychology journal on the table. "Many psychologists believe that negative, tearing-down, derogatory messages are so powerful, so toxic, they can overpower positive messages by a ratio of three or four to one. One negative comment can shoot down the good effects of three or four positive ones. To keep things in balance between the negatives and positives, the positives must outnumber the negative comments by at least three to one. People don't realize that. And yet, what do you remember when someone evaluates your performance? All the plaudits, or rather, the one little negative thing the critic came up with?"

"There are times we have to criticize our partner," Debi said.

"Some of us more than others," Brian interrupted, grinning.

Undaunted, Debi continued, "You don't just dream up shallow or artificial positive comments. You stress valid ones. A lot of people don't realize they can affirm the obvious."

Robert agreed. "I've had couples who said, 'we don't know how to encourage each other.' In one case, the woman was extremely hungry to hear that her husband appreciated her. He certainly did. It just never occurred to him to say so. He thought she'd just take it for granted. It was obvious to him; so why should she have to hear it in words? So you can find plenty of positives by identifying obvious things you value or appreciate."

"And you never lie," Debi added. "Marital fidelity. The husband is a good financial provider. The wife is a devoted mother, whatever—but your encouragement must be true."

Brian finished her thought (he does that sometimes). "And that's not as hard as it sounds. We all have a tendency to zoom our critical radar right in on the trouble spots, the stuck places. If thirty percent of your marriage is lousy, that's seventy percent that's good. It's there somewhere."

"We often," Robert interjected, "counsel couples to establish both formal periods and spontaneous episodes of affirming and encouraging. I suggest to couples who have trouble building each other up to set aside a time of day to do it. Like the last five minutes before going to bed. Each person takes a couple minutes to affirm what they like and value about each other. Affirm something they noticed during the day, or fall back on an obvious. I had one couple who were so structured they used an egg timer. After they did that for a month or two, they could scale back and make it less structured. But they were so hungry and so unaccustomed to being encouraged, they needed the structure at first."

"Formal or informal," Brian agreed. "As a rule, I suggest it's usually best to keep it one-sided; positive strokes and not negative."

"Not that we're ignoring negative aspects or denying them . . ."

"Absolutely not. But this is build-up time. Give your partner some unconditional acceptance, love, confirmation . . ."

Debi finished his thought for him; "Endorsement, affirmation. Approval without amendment. One other thing I suggest to people is, try to see your spouse as the world does."

"Oh, yes!" Robert Hemfelt gestured enthusiastically. "How many times have you heard, 'All of my friends love my husband, but they don't have to put up with him at home.' "

"Often there really is a different side of him when he comes home. People change when they walk in the front door."

"That's right. I tell clients, we are not asking that you be blind to your spouse's negative side. There is a place and time to confront that. But when he steps in the door can I try to focus on the positive qualities even if he doesn't bring them home, those qualities that other people admire are positive out in the world? If your person is well-liked, look why. What's the positive?"

"Or positives," Debi added. "Almost always there are several or many. None of this is a license to deny the negative or ignore it, just put it in its place. It's three-to-one place."

Ilona Guthrie was coming from behind in this area of building up her mate, way behind. She carried little or no respect at all for her bumbling husband. She had soured so much that, in her eyes, he had no valid position. Once she realized that, she saw also how she had to quit carping and start encouraging him; the way things were going so far would lead to disaster.

He was getting all kinds of good strokes from the outside world. People left cookies for him when he delivered goods near Christmas time. The 4-H leaders praised him to the skies. The church deacons spoke highly of him. At home, Ilona crabbed about his slipshod ways, or ignored him altogether. Hardly a buildup.

She made a conscious, determined decision to start accepting Reede unconditionally, warts and all. Okay, so some of the stuff he did irritated her to no end. She would accept it.

She would forgive him, daily if need be, for the things he neglected or did wrong. And she would forgive herself when she let some irritation get to her. She had to learn to laugh off some of it.

At her Bible study group Ilona and her friends studied the ideal woman of Proverbs 31. "She does him good and not ill all her days." Here was a busy woman who put her husband's best interests first. Ilona always put the kids first. Indeed, she took care to encourage the children, but she never bothered to encourage Reede; she hadn't noticed that before.

How do you encourage your mate without sounding a little foolish? Ilona started out small. In her Bible study group, during their praise session at the beginning of each meeting, she praised the Lord for something positive about Reede. Thus emboldened, she could work her way up to praising Reede to his face. Pretty soon she was praising him in front of the kids. That had never happened before. Did he soak it up? Does a dog lap water?

Ilona made another list. At least twice a week she'd find occasion to do several things. She would definitely do something for Reede. Do what? Something; let the moment decide. She would bite her tongue when she started to say something disparaging and try to break herself of that habit. And she would gouge out a little time to devote just to Reede, like she did for the kids and herself.

Finally, she determined to settle in for the long haul. This would be no instant zap cure, no prescription of antibiotics and presto, the infection's gone. It would take time—the rest of the marriage, probably. She prepared herself for that. But then, marriage is a lifelong job.

With no retirement plan.

Serendipity

Ilona couldn't remember exactly. Perhaps it was the morning Wayne's best friend, Andy, down the road discovered his lamb had gotten hung up in barbed wire and ripped open its leg, and Reede literally picked the squirming sheep up, lifting all four feet up off the ground, and held it at an angle so Andy could carefully cut and unwind the wire. Loading and unloading a truck all day sure does make a body strong. Or maybe it was when Old Nasty Craig, the crotchety geezer who ran the mini-mart on the corner by Shaw's, deliberately shortchanged Jeffrey, saying the kid gave him a one when it was a ten, and Ilona wasn't getting anywhere arguing with him because she *knew* it was a ten, and instead of waiting out in the car the way he always did, Reede came inside and took Ilona's side and in no uncertain way made an honest man of Old Nasty. Or possibly it was when, on their fourteenth anniversary, Reede took her out to dinner and bought her flowers and said, "I don't understand the change, but it's wonderful. I love you, Ilona."

No matter. Whatever the exact occasion, there was a day, a moment, when Ilona Guthrie fell back in love with Reede.

Chapter 5

Can You Truly Forgive?

"**I** forgive you for hitting your sister yesterday," Ilona Guthrie stood behind eight-year-old Jeffrey in the middle of their living room.

"Uhhh, thanks Mom. I think." Jeffrey answered. He gave her a strange look and ran outside.

Reede Guthrie stared at his wife from the closet where he was hanging up his coat.

"What was that all about?" he asked.

"Isn't it wonderful. It's the very first time I can remember saying 'I forgive you' to one of the kids. I feel so much better." Ilona answered.

"But Jeffrey didn't know what you were saying. I don't think he felt much better." Reede said.

"I know. But it doesn't matter. I do." Ilona popped a quick kiss on her husband's cheek and went into the kitchen.

Reede Guthrie scratched his head and looked outside at his son playing ball in the front yard. He shrugged his shoulders and followed Ilona into the kitchen. "But Ilona, I don't understand. . ."

The Need to Forgive

Who are the people who say, "I'll never forgive," "It's too great; I cannot forgive that"? They are the ones with ulcers, high blood pressure, and tense relationships. Failure to forgive is poor physiology as well as poor theology (the Lord's Prayer specifically says, "Forgive us our trespasses as we forgive those who trespass against us"). It is also very poor psychology.

To not forgive is to do one's self in.

Passage Three presents a special challenge related to the issue of forgiveness because couples in this passage have been together long enough to have accumulated some major resentments from the first two passages. As the couple enters the Third Passage, these unresolved resentments can threaten to push the marriage to a breaking point.

The Results of Anger

The opposites of forgiveness are resentment and anger.

Anger and resentment, though, are secondary. Beneath them lies hurt—pain and the fear of pain.

See a child run carelessly into the street. The distraught parent yanks the child back to the sidewalk and scolds him angrily. Why angrily? Nothing happened; nothing was lost. Fear of the pain of loss, fear of what could have happened triggered that anger. In a marriage also, anger and resentment are born of either being hurt or the fear of being hurt.

The bugaboo here is that anger and resentment quench intimacy. If you fear being hurt by this person, you cannot feel comfortable close to this person. The fear and anger may or may not be a direct response to something your spouse is doing. In fact, your anger may have roots in pain from the family history.

One of our patients told us, "My mom was sick a lot while I was growing up. She couldn't care well for her children or participate in their raising the way most mothers did. I got tired of Mom being ill. I came to resent it, and got angry. In my marriage, when my wife was ill, I found myself minimizing her illness and getting angry about it. It was a holdover from my youth, unresolved anger, something I had to work through."

We can build another formula from this:

unresolved anger = bitterness

Put another way:

anger turned sour = bitterness

Bitterness quickly and coldly quenches love and intimacy. The final fruit of bitterness is hatred.

Every married couple must, therefore, master the ability to forgive, especially since forgiveness is an essential part of the grieving process. It's a skill that must be practiced daily, for man and wife are constantly exposed to little hurts and major problems. In order to practice this skill of forgiveness, you must be able to identify the sources of your anger.

The Sources of Anger

"Where does your anger come from?" we ask each couple we counsel. "What is its source?"

"From him!" she always insists.

"From her!" he always responds.

It is amazing how often those answers are false. But the truth lies hidden, covered by layers of denial. Are any of the following factors sources of your anger?

The In-laws

"Yes!" agrees Dave, the clergyman in our counsel. "They can really come between Genie and me." Dave may be right, but he's not right in the way he thinks he is.

"Genie worked a long time dealing with her family-of-origin issues," we told Dave. "How about you?"

"Yes, I've worked through them."

"And you found out there were some serious lacks in your childhood; things you needed that didn't happen as you were growing up."

"Well, some."

"So, in the dream-quest for perfect parents, you thought your in-laws, Mr. and Mrs. Petronavich, would be all the things your own parents were not. And when the Petronavichs fell short, you projected all that loss onto them."

"No. I don't think so."

We weren't asking Dave; we were telling him. But we didn't say that. Instead, we worked with him until he himself realized that was what he had done.

Anyone not dealing with family-of-origin issues (that is, unfinished business, lack of nurturing and such) is going to have in-law trouble. If there are lingering issues between you and your own mom and dad, you might unknowingly transfer those issues onto in-laws, thinking your brand new parents will make up for all you lacked in the past. This is a big reason there are so many in-law jokes. Ninety percent of it is projection. Dave's problem was not his in-laws, but his denial, projecting problems with his parents onto the luckless Petronavichs.

It works the other way too. In-laws who didn't resolve their own issues often transfer them onto the kids.

How do you know it's happening? If you suffer chronic, constant anger, resentment, and tension with your in-laws, projection may be involved. That's how to recognize it.

Hidden Agendas

Hidden agendas can be intense sources of anger. You may have to dig deep to find them, and you may have to change your attitudes and methods if forgiveness in your family-of-origin was inadequate.

Look into your own past, into your childhood. How was forgiveness practiced and carried out in your family-of-origin? Ask yourself two questions:

1. "Who was expected to ask for forgiveness for transgressions in your family?"
_____ Father only as head of the house?
_____ Mother only?
_____ Only children who did something wrong—never grown-ups?
_____ Whoever did the deed that needed to be forgiven?
_____ Any of the above?
_____ Nobody. We never thought about forgiveness.

2. "What was our family's attitude toward forgiveness?"
_____ Everyone was required to forget about an accident or transgression, at least on the surface, once it was forgiven.
_____ The family never talked about forgiveness or what it means to forgive.
_____ Someone in the family used this phrase at least once: "I can never forgive _____ (whoever) for _____ (some transgression)."
_____ The family talked about issues that required forgiveness and tried to resolve them.

Based on what you see in your family-of-origin, identify two patterns you want to see continue in your own family. (For example, "My parents always made a point to resolve a major dispute with open expressions of mutual forgiveness.")

1. _____

2. _____

Now identify at least two things you ought to change. (For example, "My parents rarely acknowledged to us children when they had overreacted.")

1. _____

2. _____

What anger in your life might possibly point to hidden agendas and family-of-origin habits?

"In some families," Brian Newman states, "after blowups, everyone drifts off. Then they all return slowly into good graces again until the next blowup. 'I'm talking to you again,' means 'I forgive you.' But the forgiveness isn't actually done or spoken. Putting it behind is not forgiving, per se. Calming down is not dealing with it. We must be willing to go back, address, and resolve the issues, or they'll just keep reappearing."

"Persons with low expectations and passive personalities tend to adjust to the dominant person in the family," Debi explains. "The dominant one is usually the most selfish. When the dominant one does something wrong, the more passive members are expected to forgive and forget without mentioning it. We see this especially in dynamics between parents and children, but also between dominant and passive spouses.

"What's sauce for the goose is sauce for gander; the trick is to recognize what's happening. Both the dominant and the passive personalities must seek forgiveness. Probably what attracted these two to each other was their unchangeable characteristics. We're not saying to put aside dominance or passivity here. We're saying both persons must change somewhat, move closer center of this polarity teeter-totter."

Your Spouse

Person + person = conflict. It's unavoidable.

The Expected Response

Expected by whom? By God. When Peter asked how many times one ought forgive, Jesus answered, seventy-times seven, meaning in the vernacular of that day not so much four-hundred and ninety times as an endless number of times. Even taken literally, we're talking daily forgiveness here. That whole passage, Matthew 18:21–35, is most instructive regarding God's attitude toward forgiveness.

What Forgiveness Is and Is Not

We hear frequently from our clients, "No. Even if I did forgive, I couldn't forget."

" 'Forgive and forget' may be a catchword," we reply, "but forgiving is not forgetting. Forgiveness does not mean no memories. It means we choose not to go through life bitter." You can accept the forgivee's mistakes, choose to forgive, and still find yourself talking about what happened.

Nor should forgiveness be instantaneous. Somehow, the forgiver has the idea that once forgiveness has occurred, all those angry, hurt feelings will melt away. Then the forgiver feels guilty, for that very rarely happens. Forgiveness is not a once-and-done bandage over the wound.

You are commanded to forgive. That means you are not supposed to wait for your feelings. It's a considered decision. It is not a single act but a process. Compare forgiveness with salvation. You come to know, which is a cognitive decision with or without emotions. As you learn more, it then becomes a felt thing. Ultimately, it becomes part of you. This is a part of what Paul talks about when he urges us to the renewal of our mind in Romans 12:2.

Forgiving, however, is easier said than done. That's why learning how to truly forgive is the fourth task of this Third Passage of marriage.

The Fourth Task: To Practice True Forgiveness

"How to forgive? Easy," said Ilona Guthrie. "You tell the person to their face, 'I forgive you.' "

Would that it were so simple. Strong, healthful, effective forgiveness requires six steps.

First, Acknowledge and Admit Your Hurts

"That's easy," said Ilona. "Reede's a bumbling idiot. Everything he touches turns to disaster. I'm constantly putting out his fires. In the bedroom? Hah! Same ol' Reede. Predictable, boring. Our marriage just sits there—like Reede does in front of the television. The only thing that keeps me interested is the kids."

"Very well. List all the items—every annoyance and error. Write it in the form of a letter, if you wish, although your mate may not know about it. Articulate your feelings and thoughts. Some of our clients tape record the letter or dictate it. The whole idea is to help identify the hurt and pain in life. Be thorough and painstaking with this letter. By the time a couple reaches Passage Three, there may be significant hurts in at least three areas:

1) Disappointed dreams: Perhaps your husband promised you he would own his own business by the time you reached midlife. Midlife is here and he is still working for someone else.

2) Annoying habits: You may be frustrated because your wife was fifteen to twenty minutes late for every date during your courtship. You were certain she would change this habit after you married. Now, in Passage Three, she is fifteen to twenty minutes late for every family event.

3) Unresolved hurts: You may recall an eight-month period before your tenth anniversary when your husband would neither touch you nor initiate sex. You didn't understand it then, and the memory still hurts you now.

When you have a clear picture of exactly what should be forgiven, grieve the pain they caused, then burn the letter, the paper."

"You're kidding! Burn the paper? Don't show it to him?"

"There is a time and place to confront ongoing hurt and abusive behaviors. That will come later. You're inventorying what has not yet been forgiven. This is an effort at self-honesty about what needs to be forgiven."

"Yes, but burn it?"

"The burning symbolizes your willingness to release the old hurt. You will be acting as God has toward us. Our debt to God is infinitely greater than anything our spouses could do. But God has forgiven us and released His hurt."

"Well, yeah, but. . . "

The six of us are all firmly convinced, based on our faith and our experience, that only a solid relationship with God provides the freedom to forgive. Put differently, no true forgiveness occurs without a relationship with God, because apart from God there is no real understanding of forgiveness.

Second, Commit to Forgiveness

"If I weren't committed to it, I wouldn't try," Ilona insisted.

"We mean, settling in for the long haul," we replied.

Forgiveness doesn't erase the past or the effects of the past. Forgiveness must be maintained against the intrusions of the past, and that requires commitment. With commitment, you can battle resurfacing memories of past hurt and the day-to-day encounter with your spouse's hurtful imperfections—imperfections that may never change.

Also, you cannot focus on your feelings or you'll never forgive. You can't wait to feel better about it, or to somehow feel forgiving, because with every hour you wait, bitterness is festering. Forgiveness is a choice. After you commit to forgiveness, the mellowing feelings will eventually catch up.

Consider Randi and James. Both of them came out of conservative church backgrounds; both knew from childhood on that premarital sex is sinful. But they were young and in love and this was Today. Everyone's doing it Today. So did they. Unfortunately, years into their marriage, Randi still had not forgiven James for coercing her into premarital sexual activity. Her smoldering resentment ate into their intimacy, into their sexual enjoyment, into the delicate fabric of their marriage.

By the time they reached Passage Three, Randi was experiencing long periods of sexual frigidity and James was threatening to have an affair, even though that would violate his deepest values. We could counsel Randi in how to forgive, using these six steps.

We could encourage her to grieve the losses her resentment caused. But she had to commit to obeying Christ's wishes regarding forgiveness that lasts. In the process, both Randi and James had to take responsibility for premarital sex in courtship and the severe breakdown in sexual sharing in Passage Three.

Third, Be Prepared to Yield

And again we say, forgiving does not mean forgetting. But it does mean yielding up your right to retribution, and that is not an easy thing to do. When you are hurt, you want to lash back. How hard it is to deliberately choose not to demand that right! Moreover, it's not something you do grudgingly. You must voluntarily turn over to God your rights of retaliation. 'Vengeance is mine,' saith the Lord. In part, that's because He's so much better at it than you could ever hope to be.

We are not talking here about legal actions and contexts. For your own health and peace of mind you must forgive your ex-spouse; it's what God wants of you. But that does not mean you excuse that ex-spouse from child support or other appropriate legal obligations. The crime victim is called upon to forgive the criminal, but certainly not, by withdrawing testimony or charges, to stymie justice.

Because you are forgiving the person, not the act, this statement does not bear weight: "I can't condone an act like that. Forgiving means putting my stamp of approval on an unforgivable act. It makes that person look all right, and he/she is *not* all right!" Do you see the difference between condoning a possibly unforgivable act, perhaps a heinous, damaging, vicious act, and forgiving the person? Do you see the difference between the sin and the sinner? That is the difference you must make as you forgive and forgive again.

It takes strength and humility to relinquish the right of retribution, and to expose our own hurt. Too much hate gets in the way. Frankly, true, complete forgiveness is not possible in human strength. We have learned from long experience that you cannot wait for the hurt to subside; you cannot wait until a feeling of forgiveness nudges into your heart and mind. It never will. The hurt will fester. You must accept God's help by asking for His help. Call on His strength added to yours. And don't wait for a nice, warm feeling.

Attitudes are adjustable. At any given moment, with help from the Holy Spirit, a person can say "God, I want to initiate a spirit of forgiveness, now." And it does not depend on the other person.

You see, at the bottom of it, this all is intended for the forgiver's benefit, not the forgivee's. Whether or not you consciously relinquish rights of vengeance and retribution does not depend on the sinner's state of mind. He or she may or may not seem repentant. He/she may not feel sorry or even admit to the transgression. Forgiveness is *your* thing, the action taken on *your* part. Their actions and reactions are up to them.

Remember our couple, Randi and James, who were caught in a sexual impasse. Randi felt wounded by James's repeated threats to have an affair. She didn't believe he would really have one, but the threats hurt sufficiently. And James felt hurt by Randi's loss of sexual desire.

Each felt hurt by the other and was dishing out his own form of human retribution. Randi's frigidity was her body's way of saying, "I'll punish you for your threats to have an affair." And James's threats of infidelity were a cruel way of saying, "I feel sexually rejected and put down by you. For that, I'll push your most vulnerable button with my threats."

Retribution from one triggered escalated vengeance in the other. The only way out of this cycle was for one to yield the right to retribution.

If you ever doubt that you need to yield your efforts to bring about justice and yield your accumulated anger from a failure to forgive, consider the enormous toll the anger takes on your physical well-being. Most medical practitioners agree that in our modern society, up to fifty percent of physical disorders are significantly if not primarily stress-related. Anger, resentment, and fear are powerful stressors. But what is most important, they can be reduced or eliminated through forgiveness. (We recommend the book *Worry-Free Living* (Thomas Nelson: Nashville, 1989) by Dr. Frank Minirth, Dr. Paul Meier, and Don Hawkins, for a more detailed discussion of the effects of anger and other stressors.)

One final thing you must give up as a function of forgiving: "I relinquish my bitterness that you did this to me." That, too, is terribly hard to do. But it's necessary. When you deliberately put the bitterness aside, you put the issue to rest.

Fourth, Be Open to the Relationship

Because forgiveness does not erase the original offense, it is, so often, hard to warm up again to the person near and dear who wronged you. One goal of forgiveness is the full restoration of the damaged or ruptured relationship. Therefore, both partners must commit to be open to a new relationship. Forgiveness definitely means choosing not to carry a grudge. The memories remain to be worked through. Remember that the memories live in both partners. You must have time to work through your own attitudes, and you must give the person you've forgiven time and space to work through his or her hurts also.

Eleven years into their marriage, Jeff cheated on his wife Joyce with a brief fling. With difficulty, Joyce forgave him. But in a sense she held a grudge against Jeff for coming back into the marriage after so painful a transgression. Jeff had been dealing with his conscience for several months before Joyce discovered what he'd done. He had that much time to process the pain and forgive himself. Joyce was starting from day one. She needed several months longer to deal with the issue; Jeff could not expect her to be where he was in the process.

Joyce, though, could not leave it alone. Although she technically forgave Jeff, she kept punishing him by constantly bringing it up, making sure he knew he wasn't trusted, making snide comments. Here was Jeff, a better husband than he had ever been before and determined to be faithful and loving, and she was treating him worse than she had ever treated him before. She was no longer open to an intimate relationship with him, regardless what she claimed her feelings were.

It takes a minimum of several months or longer, for most persons in a ruptured marriage such as Jeff and Joyce's to get over the emotional pain enough to restore the sexual bond. Even then the pain is not put behind completely. That's just the start of their return to intimacy and trusting. The person who had the affair must be patient. We recommend the book *Broken Vows* (Thomas Nelson: Nashville, 1991) by Dr. Les Carter for couples who are struggling with marital infidelity.

There is one important exception to being open to the relationship—when one or the other spouse is blatantly abusive. We never recommend a person return to an abusive relationship until the abuser is well enough on the road to recovery that the person's health and safety are assured.

Fifth, Confess and Confront

When we began this discussion of the six steps toward forgiveness, we said there would be an appropriate time to confront your partner with painful or offending behaviors. How can you constructively confront or confess to your spouse?

It is important that you not attempt the confrontation or confession in moments of intense anger or overpowering shame. Our tendency is to want to jump into confession or confrontation. Notice, however, we are suggesting this phase of resolving pain near the end of the six steps.

Working through your own hurt feelings, surrendering your need for human retribution, and committing to the renewal of the relationship, puts you in a position to confront constructively your spouse's hurtful behaviors and to establish new boundaries to prevent future hurts. You may choose at this time to share and confess your own contribution to what has gone off track in the relationship. Your open williness to confess your own contribution to the breakdown or impasse will help pave the way for your spouse to hear your confrontation.

Choose a moment of relative calm and preface the sharing with a statement of affirmation to show you are approaching with love. For example, "I'm thankful for the strong commitment to make our relationship work, but I have to be honest with you about the extent of the hurt I feel from the past and the fear I have that this pattern will repeat itself in the future."

Often couples find it helpful to write out these confessions and confrontations. A wife may need to confront her husband about his indifference toward something major missing in their relationship.

"How do I tell him?" she asks. We advocate writing a letter. You can write down—and rewrite—precisely what you want, but when you talk, the focus almost always gets shifted. You lose your point or get off on something else or you get pushed into an immediate debate. With a letter there is less chance of miscommunication.

Give your spouse that letter when the person doesn't have to be defensive, can read it in a non-threatening atmosphere, has no need to respond back immediately. Let the person have all the time needed to reread it, study it, think about it, feel through it.

This sort of confession obviously involves confrontation. What should you do if your mate denies the reality of the situation, refuses to talk about it, or counterattacks with massive anger? That happens so much.

Let's go back to Randi and James, and pretend that James absolutely denied that anything was wrong. He categorically refused to consider Randi's anger and resentment. "Just a hysterical woman looking for an excuse to be crabby," he'd say, and brush it off.

Randi's first step would be acknowledging her anger, to herself as much as anyone. She would write a letter telling about it. She'd pour her heart out (and almost always, when a person does this, that person is shocked by the stabbing intensity of his or her feelings). Then she'd rewrite the letter into something James could read. She would explain how her anger was eating at her. She would tell how she wanted to restore their relationship to one of love and enjoyment.

Now, understand that because forgiveness is based not on the other person's responses but upon one's own needs, Randi would not have had to write those letters in order to forgive. She has already worked on the internal dimensions of forgiveness in her previous steps.

Whether James responded or not to Randi's letter, Randi would have done her part by acknowledging her hurt and forgiving him. She was sincere in her efforts to restore the relationship. If James still failed to acknowledge a problem, it would become his problem, not hers.

At times it's impossible to talk to the offender because that person is dead or out of contact. Perhaps you are divorced and didn't work through forgiveness with your ex until now. You're carrying unresolved anger. That anger affects how open you are to intimacy with others, for unresolved issues—and anger is only one of many—close a person off to other intimacy. When contact is impossible, it behooves you to sit down and work through the issues by recognizing your anger, grieving the losses, and forgiving.

Put It Behind

We talked about forgiving and forgetting being two different things. You've forgiven. Now, if possible, forget. If that's not possible, don't blame yourself. Scripture says that God literally forgets our sins and transgressions once we've sought out His forgiveness. But there are only two verities in the world: 1) there is a God, and 2) you are not Him. Human beings, being human, cannot often erase memories.

Although the memories of past hurts cannot be fully erased, you do have the option, the choice, by God's empowerment to put the past behind and to open a fresh new chapter on your relationship together. Opening this new chapter through in-depth forgiveness in Passage Three will set the stage for other forms of relationship renewal in Passage Four.

Barriers to Forgiving

"This guy must have been coming down the grocery store aisle at a dead run," Ilona Guthrie recalled. "One minute the aisle's clear and the next moment he's slamming into me. Bowled me over, knocked me down—I'm just lucky I didn't crash into one of those canned food displays and send cans everywhere. He was *so* apologetic. He said he was trying to catch his wife before she left the store—something like that—and wasn't watching where he was going."

"You forgave him?"

"Sure. I've done stuff like that plenty of times. I understood. Forgiving him wasn't difficult at all."

"Perhaps," we suggested, "forgiving was easy because he was a total stranger."

Ilona stared at our wall for a few minutes. "That's true. I never thought of that. If it had been Reede who knocked me down like that I still wouldn't be speaking to him."

It's So Hard to Forgive Those Closest to You

The people we're most likely to be bitter with, the people who most need to be forgiven, are those closest to us. Husband, wife, parents, these are the persons we most need to forgive, for if we don't, we can't hope to work through the passages of marriage.

And yet, they are the persons, of all people in the world, we find hardest to honestly forgive.

Ilona saw her own weakness in that stranger, and recognized that she quite as easily could have been the one knocking someone else down. Had it been Reede, she would only have condemned his carelessness. There's a clue here, you see: If you can remember that no one is perfect—not your mate, not your parents, certainly not yourself—you will enjoy greater freedom to forgive.

We have talked at great length about how hidden agendas can be passed on to you from your parents or even your grandparents. Now is the time to forgive them for this baggage they sent with you. It helps no one, especially you, to hold a grudge against your parents. Give them the benefit of the doubt. They may well have done the best they could under the circumstances. Remember they also received baggage from their parents and grandparents. Recall you are forgiving the persons, not the acts. Your parents may well have invoked serious abuse and neglect. Again, this forgiveness is for your benefit, as well as a benefit for the next generation. Only by forgiving them and grieving your losses can you prevent this same baggage from being passed on to your own children, and even your grandchildren.

Give the folks a break, welcome them as friends—"equals" in your life as we mentioned in Chapter 3. Forgive them their transgressions in your childrearing, and get on with your life. Work on those hidden agendas and problems. Take responsibility for your own actions and forgive yourself.

You are the one person even more difficult to forgive than spouses or parents. In this case, your self-talk gets in the way. You become angry with yourself, castigating yourself about how stupid you are, what others must think about you. If you are typical of people we know and counsel (and we ourselves), you are much harder on yourself than you would be on someone else. You wouldn't talk to another person the way you self-talk. You certainly wouldn't think that aloud to your best friend. Watch, therefore, for lack of forgiveness toward yourself. Talk to yourself as you would to a treasured friend, forgive your own mistakes, and move on.

And then there's God. When have you forgiven God lately?

"Now you really are kidding!" Ilona exclaimed. "God is perfect. He doesn't do anything to be forgiven for."

"True in theory," we reply, "but the heart doesn't deal in theories."

In reality, persons often hold a grudge against God because, being human, they lack the intelligence and foresight to understand why God did a particular thing. It seems so useless, so senseless, so damaging. Why did so-and-so die, or I get sick, or that tragedy come to pass? Try as you might, you can see only a tiny smattering of what He has in mind. This is a poor comparison, because God is so far above us, but think how often a small child cannot perceive what you do or feel, because he simply doesn't have the ability to understand.

In forgiving God, then, we end up not forgiving Him for His shortcomings but for ours. Again, forgiveness benefits the forgiver infinitely more than the forgivee. If you feel a need to forgive God His inscrutability, by all means do so.

False Forgiving

"When problems are stuffed and frictions put away without dealing with them," Brian Newman says, "there is a sense of false forgiveness. The issues aren't brought out, the forgiveness never spoken."

False, too, is the temptation to say "I forgive you" as cheap words to get the argument ended or to gloss over painful or difficult issues. Those simple words must be said with meaning for forgiveness to be real.

Often in counseling we see codependents attempt false forgiveness. Afraid they'll be rejected if they rock the boat, they'll say anything, then stuff their true feelings away inside. This denial of authentic feelings is oftentimes called codependent people-pleasing. You can stuff just so many feelings into a pained heart before something explodes. Stored emotions become bitterness. They will come out as passive aggression, as depression, as anxiety, as physical symptoms. True forgiveness requires that you acknowledge the pain that person's act has caused your heart, but in so doing you commence the healing process.

We often find false forgiveness cropping up in the early years of marriage. The relationship is not fully in place, and both persons lack the security of knowing each other well. In these newlywed years, too, both are convinced that if we're truly in love, we shouldn't have to forgive anything. Oh, we shouldn't have conflicts! Without fully realizing it, we sweep everything under the carpet.

If enough hurts have been swept under the carpet through false forgiveness in Passages One and Two, the couple may find themselves at a full-blown relationship standoff in Passage Three. It takes courage and faith to be willing to reverse old patterns of burying signgicant hurts and needs and to confront honestly these issues in Passage Three as a building block of authentic forgiveness and new intimacy.

True love is *constantly* having to say you're sorry.

Results of Forgiving

Loren and Gayle had been married thirteen years, and they fought constantly. Sometimes she'd walk out. Usually they simply resolved the conflicts by ceasing fighting, often upon the urging of well-meaning friends who wanted to see them stay together. What they were actually doing was putting the issues aside. The issues, you see, were still available, ready to resurface at any time. Loren and Gayle's fighting lost or gained intensity from time to time, but it was always there. Nothing they fought over was resolved. They never examined the issues, and they never ever forgave.

Did Loren and Gayle have a satisfying marriage? They thought so. They didn't like the fighting, but what can you do? Their differences were irreconcilable, and you know what irreconcilable differences can lead to.

Relief came, eventually, when their friends finally got them into counseling. We helped them acknowledge that they were never resolving anything. Putting a fight aside is not dealing with it, any more than Brian's family dealt with issues by parting in silence a while. In Loren and Gayle's case, healing commenced when they brought the issues out, examined the past to see where they originated, and then forgave each other the hurt and irritation. For six months thereafter, they would drop notes or call, telling in glowing terms about the latest forward step into further intimacy.

An issue forgiven is an issue at rest. The anger may not be resolved, and certainly not forgotten. But the issue itself will not be brought up again, having been literally laid aside. Dennis Raney and others call the stuff you drag out later "bazookas in the closet."

Unresolved anger damages intimacy; forgiveness mends it.

Without forgiveness you can get stuck in any passage. When people mature and change (and when a marriage matures and changes), they inadvertently step on each other's toes. Moreover, married people make mistakes which require forgiveness, sometimes in megadoses. Until the mistakes and issues of one passage are resolved, the couple cannot move on to the greater intimacy and new horizons the next passage introduces.

But there's far more. Forgiveness offers freedom from guilt, resentment, hostility, and bitterness. "I will never allow another person to ruin my life by hating them," said George Washington Carver.

By forgiving, you allow God's love to shine before your spouse. But there's even more.

We cannot have intimacy with God except that He forgave us and thereby broke away the wall of sin between us and Him. Jesus in the fifth chapter of Matthew instructs His followers to leave their gift to God on the altar if they have a point of friction with another. He says to go to that person and deal with the problem; only then is the believer prepared to give a gift to God. By forgiving, you do your part toward laying the problem or point of friction to rest. You thereby prepare yourself to freely enjoy a close relationship with your Lord.

What greater reward can there be?

Chapter 6

Are You Prepared for the Inevitable Losses?

"Mid-life is horrible! It's horrible. Life was going along pretty good, everything going well, kids fine, marriage good. . . I hit mid-life, one parent died, aunts and uncles died, my father-in-law died, a child got ill, my own health faltered. Mid-life is tough.

"You change positions. No longer is there anyone to look to. There's no dad there, no mom to take care of you. No one there to wipe away the tears. You can no longer go to the parents. They took care of you, now you're gonna take care of them or at least have to stand on your own. In a sense you don't totally lose it all; they are with you in mind and memory, but not in the practical everyday. You move into the final position as the elder, the grown-up, the one to be depended upon, which is frightening; it's a tough transition emotionally. You're not only saying good-bye, but taking on roles and responsibilities you never had before or even thought about.

"Fortunately, the body of Christ is broad, and God uses other members of the body to support you, but it's a change in your support base, all the same.

"Young love is great. Your twenties were great as you firmed up your commitments, laid out goals. You decided how your own family would run. The thirties are tremendously productive, high-energy years. Then the forties. You can't see as well, your elder relatives are starting to die, you yourself are slowing down physically. . . . Mid-life is tough. In my opinion, maybe one of the worst stages."

Whose opinion? Dr. Frank Minirth's. The man who gave talks on beating the odds—the farm boy who completed medical school, his residency, and seminary; the diabetic who lives his life a day at a time—suddenly found the odds taking a turn against him.

You, too, are fighting the odds by this stage of marriage. So much is at stake, just as your capabilities crest the hill and start their inexorable roll down the sunset side.

Crisis and Change

"How did I ever let myself get talked into this?" your mind screams as you look up the forbidding face of a cliff in El Dorado Canyon, Colorado. You always wanted to climb and now here you are, coerced into this activity by your "good" friend. At the same time, your adrenaline rushes throughout your bloodstream. You cannot recall a time when you felt so energized.

"On belay," you call out. Your friend answers, "Belay on." The rope tightens on your harness urging you upward. But to where? Your hands sweat, you reach into your chalk bag. Then you feel the relief of the rock face in front of you. Your concentration is centered on this microenvironment. Ah ha! A ledge over to the right, you stretttcchh your leg over and push up with your foot. Where to put your hand? Another ledge. You brush away the dust and hook your fingers in, pulling yourself up with the help of your foot. Now where? The choices are endless. If you go to the left, there's a difficult overhang. To the right, a crack, but you have to move horizontally a few feet. Up, you see minuscule bumps and ledges. Down? Nooo! Don't look down, have to go up.

Life in this Third Passage provides just as many routes. Some of the routes you could take lead to better routes, more options. Many dead end. Here it is so easy for people swamped by decision-making to simply get stuck on a ledge.

Dr. Deborah Newman points out, "You can't be asking questions about mid-life now, and reevaluating. The time for questions is done. You're there. This is now the time of either crisis or growth, a major, major fork in the route of decisions. Crisis will either destroy you or generate new intimacy and growth."

Remember that crisis is not necessarily a burst of anger and panic. Crises can also come and go silently, leaving behind not conflagration but quiet desperation. The issues of mid-life are coming on stronger now, more demanding, more immediate; unless they've been resolved in the past, they're looming much bigger. Divorce is a too-frequent outgrowth of not making it through this difficult mid-life passage.

This is a reason there are so many mid-life sexual affairs. People can't cope with all the pressing changes, so they try to cope with surface issues. Find someone young, shift attention from the painful realities to a less painful fantasy, renew your own aging body with someone more youthful-looking and attractive. The divorce rate is not necessarily higher at this stage. Many people, miserable with their dead dreams, simply have not bothered with the actual legal steps; they've divorced in spirit though not in act.

Not all dreams have died. By mid-life now you may be living many of your dreams—if not exactly, at least close. This is the passage also where lovers can really start growing. This is where they either renew love or live in the pits. Too often, usually for lack of the effort to change, couples live in the pits unless something jolts them into revitalizing their love.

Working with you are memories and history. You've made it this far, despite some ridiculous escapades. The end is worth shooting for! Perhaps it's even worth shooting for with gusto.

The Differing Ages of the Third Passage

It is worth noting at this point that not everyone saddled with Third Passage problems (and blessed with its joys!) have actually entered this Third Passage chronologically. Some persons, marrying late, telescope the passages, though not by choice. More of life seems to happen to them more quickly.

These days, people in their mid or late thirties are having babies the same as the twenty-year-olds. Parents of same-age kids will be a decade apart in age. That's not negative, but it changes the marriage passages picture a bit. These people who are getting a late start will be hit by factors of different passages all at once.

Susan and Robert Hemfelt married when she was twenty-seven and he thirty-two. "If you have later-life babies," Susan explains, "your family will feel more stress. The kids are growing, too young yet to be out on their own—sometimes even too young yet for school. At the same time, your parents are getting sick, possibly dying. The frustration is multiplied when parents and adult children aren't geographically located in the same area.

"Take, for example, a woman in her early forties with several pre-school children. Also, her aging parents are very sick. She spends her weekends going out of town to help them; the other siblings share the responsibilities; she doesn't have to shoulder it alone, praise God. Yet she's being torn."

Older people are also more likely to move quickly through the passages themselves for several reasons. They want to be at the same place as people who married younger, and they're more mature to start with. They have a strong personal identity. They've been out on their own a while.

Susan says, "My generation is going through control issues, starting a family, and tackling third-passage issues—all that simultaneously. We're not taking the burdens and responsibilities in order. I had my first child at thirty, and then three, bam bam bam."

Added burdens and responsibilities add up to greater stress. But there's a plus side to starting out later. As Susan explains, "If you're older, and more mature, you can handle added pressure better when you get all that at once. I was already established in my career, when we married, and Robert had his underway. We had both finished our education, and were working a while; we had our careers in hand. I had confidence that if I didn't like where life was taking me, I could change it. I couldn't have had that assurance earlier. So I didn't feel trapped. A lot of friends who married young did feel trapped.

"Also, a crisis in your twenties is merely something you roll with in your thirties. You're mellowed out more. You can tap into the experiences of others because you've been around longer and seen more. It's easier to see how others did and did not do things. You're calmer, more resigned. You've seen friends go through it. Maybe what they did didn't work at all. . . or someone did so and so and it worked well. . . ."

Susan notes that she is better able to handle the stresses of a later marriage because Robert listens to her. (He does not always respond the way she thinks he ought, but he listens. And that in itself is reassuring.) But her observation brings up another point. Life and marriage are a little different for people who got started late with the process.

All couples in this passage, however, face the realities of middle age, which causes us all to pause and take note of where we are and where we are going. The fifth task of the Third Passage is to accept the losses surfacing now.

The Fifth Task: To Accept the Inevitable Losses

Four friends sat around discussing just when they truly realized in their hearts that they weren't young anymore.

"I watched the Mousketeers when I was a little kid," said one. "Jimmy Dodd. Annette and Tommy and all them. I felt suddenly terribly old the day I heard two of the Mousketeers had divorced."

"I was going through employment applications," said another. "This one man listed as his birthdate the day I graduated from college. 'The kid can't even get his birthday right,' I mumbled. Then I realized it was correct."

"When the salesclerks come up to you and address you as 'Madam' instead of 'Miss.' "

"When my hairdresser stopped cracking her gum long enough to say, 'When we gonna start rinsing this gray, honey?' "

Good-bye, Lost Youth

"What has it all been about?" Marj Ajanian pondered that question aloud. "I asked myself that a million times after my kids got bigger. I didn't have any use anymore. Maybe I never did; if I hadn't raised my kids, someone else would have, and maybe better than I did. Then I married Louie, and I had a reason again. And yet, it wasn't a really good reason. A woman's supposed to be more than just a sidekick for a man. Sure, I worked my whole life, but where's something to show for it?"

Men feel the emptiness, too, as they face aging and their waning sexuality. A man wants to be interesting to young women. He innately yearns to charm cookies, not dog biscuits. And we've found that our patients pretty much all are aware of the way modern American culture emphasizes youth over wisdom and blatantly encourages everyone to diligently fight any sign of aging. All that cultural emphasis makes the job of acceptance extremely difficult.

Not long ago a woman named Darla went to a plastic surgeon seeking breast augmentation. She was in her mid-thirties and her breasts sagged. The surgeon suspected hidden motives, anticipated that she would probably be disappointed with the results, and sent her to a psychologist first. Thus did she arrive at our clinic.

At Darla's age, her mother had gained sixty pounds, letting herself go. Dad, disgusted, divorced her when Darla was still a teen. The mother's fear and vulnerability about aging had spilled into Darla, fostering her excessive concern about her physical appearance. Her husband repeatedly reassured her that he loved her as she was and was very cool toward breast surgery. Darla then began to wonder, "If I'm not doing it for my husband or my marriage, why am I doing it?" She went back and grieved the pain of losing Dad. She grieved the inevitable loss of youth.

This time she grieved it all completely. Before, she had hung up in the bargaining stage. Her preoccupation with plastic surgery was her way of bargaining, her way to outmaneuver the clock. She was stuck back in the First Passage, when youth was the key to love, and stuck in the bargaining stage of grief, bargaining her way out of the aging process.

We urged her to celebrate the positives. Her husband wasn't making his emotional and sexual love contingent on some false image. That was an important point. They were entering financial security for the first time. They knew a lot more about achieving good sex than they did ten years ago. They worked better as a parenting team now. All that went with aging. In the end, she decided to put surgery on the back burner although she didn't abandon the idea completely.

Loss of youth isn't just physical. Susan recalls, "I was twenty-seven when I married, very late getting going with kids and a family. For most of my twenties I was on my own, and I wouldn't give that time up for the world. It gave me wisdom and stability I couldn't have gotten any other way. But I grieve that loss, too—not having kids earlier. I wish I could have done both. So I take care of it, put it behind me by celebrating and grieving, and don't think about it anymore."

You included the positives, we trust. Rejoice in them. Only the negatives need be grieved and resolved. Your grieving may have to be divided by topics, so to speak. Aging affects different aspects of your life. List them. Now look at the losses incurred in each aspect. You'll want to meditate upon each of them and deal with them separately.

Good-bye, Lost Health

James Jorgensen sat on his doctor's examining table wearing that ridiculous paper shirt and drape.

"Can't seem to find anything wrong here." His doctor commented looking over his chart. "Ticker's fine."

"Why the chest pain then?" James asked.

"Do you feel this pain usually after eating or at night while lying down?"

"As a matter of fact, yes."

"I'm going to ask for some tests on your gastrointestinal tract. We might be dealing with heartburn."

"Heartburn!"

We counsel every reader regardless of his or her age to stay on top of potential health problems. Keep a lid on them. Many can be minimized or even solved if caught in time. We now have the ability to live longer and more productively. Tap into it.

It is appropriate—in fact, it's essential—that you work through the reality of your fading physical vitality. Working through it involves both accepting it and grieving the losses. You need not succumb to it and give up. You should not. But neither can you glibly deny what is happening.

Improving your physical health, of course, as well as coming to grips with it, helps your marriage directly. Exercise and diet are the best ways to maintain and improve your physical health.

Accepting and embracing your waning youth is the best way to improve your mental health. The better you feel, and the better you feel about it, the less likely you will be to get trapped in the passage.

If you are in this Third Passage of marriage, or have reached that age, you are beginning to feel the effects of all those years of wear and tear on your body. Such losses are properly grieved through, as are other losses.

Let us go through the grief process again, from a somewhat different angle. We emphasize it because it is so centrally important to your negotiation of all the passages of marriage.

First, list some physical differences, both positive and negative, between your body today and what it was twenty years ago. (For example, "I know I'm carrying fifteen to twenty pounds more in my mid-section than I did twenty years ago.")

1._____

2._____

3._____

Now list some differences of performance. What is your body less capable of doing now? Is it better at some things than when you were young? (For example, "Twenty years ago, I looked forward to walking around eighteen holes of golf. Today the mototrized golf cart seems like a necessity.")

1._____

2._____

3._____

Those items that improved over the years are worthy of celebration. We always encourage patients and friends to celebrate both things that are good and things that could be better than they are. In fact, that's a good reason to celebrate in any case. Your state could be worse.

Now go through the items of loss one by one. Celebration and grief go hand in hand. Grief is as appropriate now as celebration was. Have you adequately grieved the loss of youthful health? If no such feelings come to mind, perhaps your grieving is not complete.

Can you remember feelings of shock and denial about those items of loss you listed? *(For instance, can you remember the first time you tried to look up a telephone number and had to hold the directory at arm's length to read it?):*

_____

_____

How about anger? Perhaps it was brief; perhaps it hung about your head like a cloud for years. *(Have you felt continual irritation at not being able to read maps, the writing on business cards? The anger at being unable to do something so simple?):*

_____

_____

Depression. Anger turned inward. It may come on you simply as "a bad case of the blahs." Has depression been a part of your response to the ravages of aging? *(Do you feel angry when you can't lift something because you now have a bad back? Does that anger turn to depression?):*

_____

_____

In what ways have you been bargaining with the aging process, stopping it in its tracks so to speak?

_____ Wrinkle cream?

_____ Hair color?

_____ Cosmetic surgery?

_____ Medications and vitamins?

_____ Excessive physical exercise?

Can you think of an occasion or occasions when this phase of grief loomed large in your life as the truth of aging forced itself upon you? _____

_____

After the emotions are cleansed comes resolution, forgiveness, and acceptance. The process of physical aging has been programmed into you. Every human being ages similarly though not identically.

Remember the age-guessing booth at fairs and carnivals? A rather rough-looking man with a four-day stubble would offer to guess your age within three years. If he guessed, he won and you paid him. If he was wrong, you won and he paid you. He almost always won. Why? Because age makes itself known in certain ways, and the trained eye can see those ways in every person.

In fact, the effects of aging are so uniform that a person's chronological age can be guessed within a few years. In short, God built you to grow old. In this fallen world every blessing is sullied, but it is a blessing no less. To accept that God knows what He's doing—yes, even when He came up with this aging business—provides a wonderful freedom from anxiety and despair.

That is our attitude of resolution as we come to terms with God's inevitable process. What is yours?

The final good-bye needs to be said to those dreams you've nourished since childhood. Your answer to the question, "What are you going to be when you grow up?"

Good-bye, Vocational and Financial Dreams

By the Third Passage, most couples must face and accept certain limitations on their financial and vocational achievements. "Is this all there is?" they ask themselves. "Is it all worthwhile?"

Lost dreams forge great bitterness. To paraphrase the words of a retired friend of the Minirths': "When I graduated from high school I was going to change the world. By the time I finished college I hoped to make my mark in America. In graduate school, I thought I might change a little of Arkansas. Now I'd be content to redecorate my office."

Rare is the person who meets or exceeds the dreams of the beginnings of life. All the rest of us mourn shattered hopes. We wanted our kids to be farther above average than they are. We wanted to be higher up the vocational ladder and more elevated in the community than we are. We have regrets. Too much of life is gone and not enough has been accomplished. Those are the generalities. For the moment, ponder the specifics of disappointments in your life, and of things yet undone. You will, we hope, plan to focus in the long run on the successes.

What is a dream of yours that you fulfilled? (For example, "It was very important for me to start a business of my own, and I have done that.")

_____

What is a dream as yet unrealized? (For example, "I dreamed that my business would expand into multiple locations. I'm still in the one single shop and that's how it looks it's going to remain.")

_____

Do you still plan to fulfill it? _____yes _____no
What is a situation others might consider a dream come true that happened to you although you never anticipated it?

_____

When you first married, what did you think your income would be by now (factoring in inflation)? $_____
If you haven't yet peaked out, can you achieve that figure?
_____yes _____no

Speaking of things undone, put a magnifying glass to your career or job. Have you advanced as far as you wish? "Job" includes domestic responsibility, the woman or man who stays home with the kids. She/he's working just as surely as the office executive, and his/her job is far less routine and predictable. If you work in a competitive environment, younger hustlers may be out to supplant you. What, if any, writing do you see on the wall?

If you have failed to reach your vocational or financial goals to date, and especially if you've reached them or nearly so, and then slid back because of today's financial climate, there is cause for grief.

First look at the disparities between your hopes and your realizations. Then, following the progression of grief steps outlined earlier, identify the shock and denial (that's important here, the denial). You may be suffering depression right now because of your unresolved hopes and dreams, but that's not the same as a temporary depression induced by the grieving process (remember the definition of depression? Anger turned inward).

A caution about the bargaining aspect of grieving: Bounce your plans off someone else, preferably a trusted associate other than your spouse. Remember, bargaining joins with wishful or magical thinking here: "If only I earn fifty dollars a week extra, I will _____." That might be a sound, reachable goal, or it might be magical thinking. Ask someone practical about the bargains you strike with yourself.

The Wonder Years?

The core of any marriage are the man and wife. But all around that core buzzes a potential problem—the kids. Kids, the marriage's greatest blessing, are also its biggest pain. Adolescents, who are building an adult or near-adult identity of their own, pose special problems for Passage Three. Let's examine those now.

Chapter 7

Is the Adolescent in Control, or Are You and Your Spouse?

"*H*e was as near perfect as a son gets," moaned May Lucas, "until six months ago. Now he's not worth dirt."

"James is fourteen now?" we asked.

"Almost fifteen. Thinks he's ready to tell the world where to get off. He slops around in those ridiculous clothes all the kids are wearing now. His hair was so pretty when it was cut right, dark and wavy. Not now; not dyed pink, let me tell you."

"How have you and your husband approached the problem so far?" we asked.

"LeRoy comes down hard on him. I don't agree with that at all. I think LeRoy is much too harsh. So I try to soften his hard line the best I can. We argue over it a lot. LeRoy's fed up, just fed up. He's ready to get the Army to consider drafting fourteen-year-olds. Whatever either one of us does, nothing seems to work."

"Tried bribery, restrictions, groundings, all that?"

"All that. We cut his allowance so many times it looks like cole slaw. I don't know where he's getting his money and that scares me to death."

"Won't he tell you?"

"Tell us? Hah!" May Lucas wagged her head. "He won't tell us if he's breathing or not. We can't get through to him and he won't talk to us. It's a disaster, Doctor! And I say it again, he was as near perfect as a son gets."

May Lucas and her husband were caught in the shifting sands of parenthood; they'd hit the third stage, the period of turmoil, which can be difficult for any parent.

The Period of Turmoil: Adolescence

Take all the causes of drifting and chaos that school-age youngsters generate and multiply each one. Now multiply the sum of them. Whatever school-age kids do and need, teens do and need more of. Clothes? Supplies? Medical? Transportation? Activities and organized events? Right. Now throw in dating, schmoozing at the mall, physical changes of maturation, awareness of self and of the opposite sex, the need to become independent by slow, painful degrees, increased scholastic pressures, harder moral choices, the plethora of choice in entertainment, activity, friendships, ways to get in trouble, ways to shine. Did we mention conflict and control issues. . . ?

So many crises come about the time kids enter their teens. Like any other conflicts, they can tear your whole marriage apart. Or your marriage can grow stronger as parents help each other and the kids.

We often receive couples into counseling when their teens get out of hand. May and LeRoy Lucas were typical of such couples; middle class, mainline church, mid-life. Because in many ways they illustrate problems posed by emergent teens (although no one's problems are clones of anyone else's), let us follow their progress as they work toward the sixth task of the Steadfast Love passage: to help your adolescent become an individual.

The Sixth Task: To Help Your Adolescent Become an
Individual

Some say that teens can tear a family apart. That, we have found, is not exactly true. Actually, teens put stress on every family because of the teens' own challenges and tasks. The stress is natural and necessary. The trouble that stress causes in the parents' marriage was already there, latent. The stress will rip open any unhealed wounds of the parents and reveal any passages left incomplete. Count on it.

Two central themes of growing from pre-teen to adulthood underlie everything about your teens' development—their behavior, their maturation, their problems, their victories and defeats. The better you the parent understand these central themes, the better you can help both your teens and your marriage.

Individuation and Control

The first of these underlying themes is individuation. The teen must shift his whole being from family member to solo individual, from governed to capable-of-self-government, from child-treated-like-a-child to adult-peer-of-adults. Too often, the social and legal strictures of our culture work against the child's efforts. The child is treated like a little kid one moment and like an adult the next, without rhyme or reason.

The second theme is control. It's the old question, "Who's in control here?" now revised to include the teen. Are the parents in control? Is the teen in control? Or is one parent or the other in control if the teen manages to divide the marriage team?

Resolving control issues seems like a never-ending battle between teens and parents because it is. Teens have to experiment with control issues in order to test their own abilities. The teen says, whether consciously or not, "Can I control my body? Can I control my environment? Can I make and control money?" And the biggest question is: "Do I have control over my own life?"

When we explained this to May Lucas, she nodded sagely. "I knew that. I mean, if I'd stopped to think about it, I'd know that. The control part, especially."

But therein lies the rub. The foundational tasks of both Passages One and Three of your marriage involve individuation issues for you the adults, the parents. The First Passage requires that the couple meld their singleness into a team. The Third Passage calls upon each of them to not let individual-ness get lost in the marriage union. And, the Second Passage deals heavily with control issues.

*If either or both parents have not clearly resolved the individu-
ation and control issues of their premarital lives—that is, their
families-of-origin—and of the first three passages of their marriage, they will not be able to parent their teens well now.*

As the teens bump into these universal, foundational issues of
individuation and control, they need a steady guide, a model.
Parents who have not come to terms with those issues cannot
provide the guidance. The parents are just as much at sea as the
kids. That leaves the kids without an anchor.

As the children work on their own issues of control and individuation, the exuberance of youth sets them to bouncing off
the walls, so to speak. That's healthy. But they must have solid
walls to bounce off of. Those solid walls are the steady parents,
the parents who have already dealt with the issues, both personally and as a marriage team. The parents can then set clear
boundaries. The children can then test those boundaries and
learn about themselves and the world.

Children need to separate from their families and find a niche
of their own ("individuate" is the technical term), but they also
need to be able to come home, particularly during their late
teens and early years of adulthood. We mean emotionally here
rather than residentially. A young adult sometimes covets the
advice and wisdom of a parent figure, particularly when facing
momentous decisions or tragedy. If Mom and Dad are confused
or weak about their own values, perhaps even their own individuality, once the teen takes wing, there is little to come back to.

This is true even before teens take wing. Over and over, ideally, the adolescents try on independence like a garment, see
what happens, and then come back to reaffirm and reembrace
the stronger, more positive values of the parents. If the parents'
values aren't solid, the teens find themselves in limbo.

Rarely is all this a conscious realization. "I need you to be a
guide, but when I look up I find nothing" is hardly ever a spoken feeling. It lies in the subconscious, working its influence
undetected.

Such an unconscious realization triggers anger in the child,
usually, or depression. It also generates a lot of friction. As a
tactical maneuver, the adolescent may try (again, unconsciously)
to provoke the parent into taking a stand. The child wants a solid

wall; instead he's feeling a padded cell. The potential for dangerous escalation then is unlimited. The more the teenager acts out to express all those needs and frustrations and anger, deliberately causing friction and getting into trouble, the more uncertain the parent becomes about his and her own abilities—the wall becomes still less solid, the teen bounces off it still more wildly, trying to find a firm surface. And down and down it spirals, to disaster.

How do you stop the spiral and climb back up? Two things you must do: First, understand yourself and your spouse.

Understand Yourself and Your Spouse

As the teens encounter the issues of individuation and control, their struggles will activate and bring to the surface all the old unresolved tasks and problems in their parents' past.

This is immensely important. At the very time the kids need their parents the most, the parents flounder in the same confusion the kids feel, reliving their own past problems that had never seen solution.

May Lucas grew up under an authoritarian father. Too authoritarian, in her opinion. Her LeRoy, praise the Lord, was a gentle, loving man, not the least stern or unyielding. He had one little kink, though; he had to know where she was all the time. All the time. Each bedtime, she had to recite a litany of where she would be the next day, and what she would do. The next day he might call during the day to make sure her schedule was in place. When he got home from work he unfailingly asked her where she had gone and what she had done. There was nothing accusing about his concern. He certainly did not suspect infidelity or any manner of dishonesty or cheating. But the pressure was always there; he had to know.

On the surface, May accepted his need to know. He didn't hang out at the bars, he didn't slip around, he didn't smoke or have any bad habits. He provided well for his family. She could forgive him his little peccadillo.

They had never worked it out as a control issue in their Second Passage. They had never mentioned it or discussed it in the First or Third Passages as an invasion of her autonomy. But that was only the surface. Down deep, resentment about being over-controlled boiled furiously. Now their fourteen-year-old James was fomenting open rebellion. James knew nothing about May's resentment; she herself refused to admit it. Surely there couldn't be any connection. Could there?

There certainly was. As James began maturing into adulthood, the old child roles didn't fit any more. Almost overnight he began expressing rebellion, and if you asked him why (which we did) he would say he didn't know. It was true; he didn't. James was expressing frustration at his father's iron hand (which had not changed since James was a little kid), but he was also expressing May's unacknowledged frustration. He would miss curfew, neglect chores. As LeRoy exerted more control, dealing out punishment as well as discipline, May became more lenient. Digging beneath the conscious, we revealed that May was enjoying her son's rebellion.

"That's foolishness!" May exploded. "He's driving me crazy. He's got me as scared as a rabbit in a fox den. How could I enjoy that?"

James was living out her rebellion for her; she couldn't do it, so it got passed as unfinished business to him. He was frustrated anyway, and chafing at the bit. It fit, in a twisted way, that he could take up her cause with his. Of course, then his behavior became all the more extreme.

True, May never said, "Go ahead and disobey your father" out loud. But she sent him signals so subtle, so covert, not even she noticed them. For example, when LeRoy would deny James his allowance, May would slip him some money.

Although that was the picture we uncovered, simply telling the Lucases what was going on and turning them loose would settle nothing. Head knowledge is not the solution; it is the first step to the solution. The second step is to shore up your marriage.

The Marriage Team

May and LeRoy had to look at their marriage and the way they parented as a team. May protested, "But it's James's rebellion we want to deal with, not something that's gone and done with in our marriage. Our marriage will do fine if James straightens up."

We asked, "Will your marriage survive if James continues as he's going?"

"I don't think so," she replied. "There's too much strain."

"So what we're dealing with here is adolescent rebellion."

"That's right."

"Good," we said. "And that rebellion is damaging the marriage, so we have to shore up the marriage. Then we all agree. Now, the first steps you take in changing James's behavior is to mend your own past. There is no quick fix, no other way around it. Shall we begin?"

1. The parents had to go through their own appropriate adolescent rebellion sooner or later—that is, either during their adolescence or now, in counseling. LeRoy had done so. May had not. We will not go into detail here; but in summary, we led May back in memory through her own adolescent years. She had to establish her identity apart from an authoritarian or controlling man. She did that, essentially, by affirming her individuality and giving herself permission to become her own woman.

If you have not dealt with these issues as they pertain to your individuality and your marriage, we urge you to read our first two books in this series: *New Love* (Thomas Nelson, 1993) and *Realistic Love* (Thomas Nelson, 1993), on the First and Second Passages of marriage. Or, we recommend you explore the steps to individuation in *Love Is a Choice* (Thomas Nelson: Nashville, 1989) by Dr. Robert Hemfelt, Dr. Frank Minirth, and Dr. Paul Meier, for family-of-origin issues. You must cover this essential groundwork before continuing, because:

2. The parents must have gone through enough adult individuation that they can confidently establish a strong value system of their own. To rephrase it, they must have clear boundaries around themselves, drawing a solid line between right and wrong, good and bad, satisfactory and unsatisfactory. Ethical, moral, religious, legal—values in every arena must be firmly in place. The child may or may not stay inside the lines, but the child *must* know where the lines are.

We find that, like LeRoy and May, parents' reactions to adolescent rebellion fall into one of two categories. Like LeRoy, they may overcompensate, mimicking their parents and quite frequently going to more of an extreme. LeRoy had strict up-bringing, and he tended to overcontrol James.

May illustrated a reaction formation, or inversion reaction. That's psychological language for "I move in the opposite direction of what the original model is inside me." May shifted from the tack of her authoritarian father to become extremely permissive. Her father's boundaries were rigid and narrow; she was incapable of setting any boundaries at all.

What about your parents' parenting techniques? Think of them in depth. Was there a strong difference in discipline between your mother and father? Extreme differences, such as LeRoy and May showed, indicate something was out of balance. How strongly did they adhere to a clear values system? Whether you accepted those values or not, did you understand what they were?

The next part of looking at your marriage is to look at the way you parent as a couple.

Work As Both a Parenting Team and As an Individual
Parent

What makes teen parenting so stressful? . . . other than the teens, that is. Stress comes when parents must present a united front, and yet they must relate to the children in an individual way. That's hard to do, because you must keep shifting roles, from parent to peer to parent to peer, sometimes in mid-sentence.

"Explain." May Lucas studied us suspiciously.

"Frankly," we said (in so many words), "You and LeRoy are showing how not to go about it. He leans heavily on James; you tip off the other way and treat James leniently. LeRoy cuts his allowance, so you slip him some money to make up for it. You undercut each other."

"But LeRoy's so harsh. Are you saying that's best?"

"Actually, either both parents harsh or both parents lenient is a better way than parents differing so widely."

"United front?"

"United front."

"LeRoy would never soften up just because I asked him to."

"Have you two ever discussed it?"

"Argued about it."

And we gave the Lucases an assignment. "Tonight, sit down facing each other. Each of you explain what you don't like about what you yourself are doing."

"Wait. You mean, I tell LeRoy what I think he's doing wrong?"

"No, you tell LeRoy what you think you yourself are doing wrong. Then he tells you what he thinks he himself is doing wrong; he sees himself reacting in anger without thinking, perhaps. Let him tell you. You both know the criticisms you level on each other. You've heard them often enough that you needn't repeat them now."

"That's so true." May nodded.

"You are not confronting each other. You're sharing your mutual problems and feelings of doubt. This more than anything else will remove the spirit of confrontation and replace it with a spirit of cooperation. Because your second assignment, then, will be to agree on firm, solid boundaries. Totally agree. You will have to compromise some, both of you. You'll have to give on some points completely. But when next you face James, you should have a united, unassailable plan for parenting him as a team."

We urge that when it comes to setting boundaries for teens, while it's important for both parents to voice their concerns and work to compromise, it is equally important that the teens not overhear or be privy to fights and negotiations. We do not mean that parents should never disagree or fight in front of children. Children need to see and hear that Mom and Dad can disagree and that's natural; the love stands secure. But not when it comes to setting teen boundaries. Model your conflict resolution in other issues.

May snorted. "You don't know our son. He'll think of something that isn't in the plan. Just you watch."

"Then you and your husband meet privately, beyond James's hearing, determine what to do about it and act on what you decided."

May shook her head. "James's not gonna like this at all."

Kids don't—or so they claim. In truth, for their sense of security, for a solid base, teens need desperately to feel that unity. It's emotionally very scary if one parent lays down a rule and the other undercuts, invalidates, or excuses that rule. Even if it's not actually spoken, the child can hear, "We don't know; we haven't reached a decision yet." Teens need black and white, another way of saying clear, vivid lines. The parents' indecision may lead them to extreme acting out—rebellion—trying to force the parents' hand and draw the line.

If you have teenaged children, see how well this exercise applies to you. If you do not yet, consider the questions carefully as a foretaste of what you will want to do.

1. Do your teens encounter a united team across all the major boundaries, including (but not limited to):

_____ Rules of the house (keeping a neat room, picking up clothes and towels, tidying the bathroom)?

_____ Friends; who visits and when, what behavior is acceptable and what's off limits?

_____ Curfews?

_____ Scheduling decisions: who gets the living room to entertain guests; who gets the car (and driver)?

_____ Work permits and income opportunities?

_____ The heavy questions: drugs, booze, cigarettes and grass, sex, other moral issues?

_____ Church attendance?

_____ School performance standards; a certain grade point average and/or behavioral expectation?

2. Do you and your spouse present an adequate model of shared religious faith and values system?

_____ Are your basic values (sanctity of life, honesty) in general agreement?

_____ If there are major differences in your value systems, do your children understand both systems and how they differ?

_____ Do you adequately model the exercise of religious faith, both individually and as a team? (You do not have to have identical relationships with God; you do have to respect each other's details of belief).

_____ When your children look at you and your spouse, do they see responsible adulthood?

3. Do your children know they are in a safe haven?

_____ If they encounter trouble—the law, an accident, a misunderstanding—do they feel secure enough to come to you immediately?

_____ Can they come to you with intimate problems and know their problems will reach no other ears but yours?

_____ In the last week have you and your spouse each individually praised your teen about something at least once?

_____ Frequently?

_____ Do your teens still receive appropriate physical affection, such as hugs, from both of you?

Note in that last survey question how important it is for parents to address their kids individually and as a team. A team is more than twice as protective as an individual. It is a bulwark, a solid front. And yet only an individual can lend an intimate and sympathetic ear. We advocate protection, not overprotection. You do not always feel confident about a situation; think how much more your teens may feel at sea in a threatening or unusual situation. They need to have backup; a recourse when everything goes down crooked.

As we counsel teens, over and over and over we hear how agonizing it was when they encountered a problem—pregnancy, drugs, a teacher or other adult making a sexual pass—and they felt they had no one to turn to for advice and protection. One or both parents were not there for them in a protective capacity.

In contrast, one young lady, Allison, told about an incident she experienced soon after she got her driver's license. "We're farm kids; we all live way out. One night about fifteen of us from youth group drove into town. It's almost fifty miles. Jeannie and Amy were with me in Dad's pick-up. We sat in the parking lot at the pizza place, waiting for the rest of the kids to get there, and listening to the radio. We got out and locked the doors—and there were the keys in the ignition and the radio going!

"The kids right away started thinking up ways out of it. One wanted to break the seal and lift out the back window, and one wanted to take up a collection to pay for a locksmith. They thought I was nuts and even tried to talk me out of it, but I called up Dad right away. I told him what happened. He drove in, fifty miles one way, with another set of keys. We got the truck started okay and ran the battery back up. Afterward, he thanked me for not letting the guys try to break into it; they would have messed up something for sure. And he thanked me for turning to him when I needed help."

Allison's dad did more than just be there for her when she needed him. He praised her for her good judgment by thanking her. This is so important. Teens desperately need affirmation. Their years are plagued by doubts and insecurity. What comes across as cockiness or indifference is actually fear and doubt. Praise should be both spontaneous and planned: applause and cheers at the basketball game, telling how well pleased both parents and grandparents are with the progress shown in the child's report card, praise for grooming, or attention paid the family pet.

In his autobiography, hockey star Wayne Gretsky tells that his father appeared at a hockey game in which it was anticipated that Wayne would break still another important league record. Wayne did, the game paused, and his father joined the others on the ice to congratulate him.

"Where's your wife?" people asked Walter Gretsky. "Shouldn't his mother be here for this, too?"

"She's at a junior league game cheering his brother on," Walter replied. " 'Wayne isn't the only hockey player in this family,' she says."

One or the other of them would be there. Although Wayne was essentially on his own in the big leagues at age fifteen, he knew his parents were behind him, with protection and with praise. And so did his siblings.

May Lucas studied the last question of the above exercise with a baleful eye. "I wish we could find something to praise James about. The pickings are sure slim in that department."

"Then praise the obvious," we suggested. "Is his physical growth on schedule?"

"Ahead of schedule. He's big for his age."

"Praise his growth. You mentioned you didn't like his hairstyle, but we assume he's very careful in his grooming."

"Oh very! Of course, he's real, *real* careful that all his effort doesn't show."

"Of course. How about, 'It must take you half an hour to put that hairdo together. That's a lot of patience.' Or, 'I saw you help Suzie next door. I'm proud of the way you treat women. Real grown-up.' Get together with LeRoy and figure ways to express your praise and approval on a planned, regular basis."

"Not lying, but finding things. I see." May sighed. "I didn't get any of that when I was growing up."

"Then it will be especially hard for you. That means none of this will come automatically. It may seem foreign, or even counter-productive. You'll have to force yourselves and practice doing it as individuals and as a team."

Like father, like son. There's a reason for that. As adulthood looms, adolescents even more assiduously blot up their parents' attitudes.

Parents serve as role models for individual taste and appreciation. May and LeRoy illustrate that well. May likes contemporary art. She genuinely appreciates it. LeRoy calls it "acres of blobs"; he's a Frederick Remington-Charlie Russell fan himself. Such diversity is healthy. James sees that divergent tastes can live in harmony. And he sees two parents with a mutually respected appreciation of art.

Parents modeling separate relationships with God may worship together and engage each in their own private study—or perhaps even vice versa, worshiping in different churches and studying together. What do the kids learn? "I can't do it for you. I can't do it to you. You have to approach God as an individual." Adolescents have budding spiritual awareness about this time. By example, the parents in essence are giving the kids permission to search for their own relationship with God.

"Do James and LeRoy ever go out and do things together?" we asked May.

"Not lately," she replied. "LeRoy says James has to straighten up before he'll take him anywhere."

We were quick to suggest LeRoy and James spend time together in some enterprise—attend sports, go to a movie, go fishing, catch the laser light show at the science center. We suggested that May also spend time one-on-one with James. This was not the time to wait until James shaped up, so to speak, or the time to withhold favors as if behavior were a condition for love and affection.

James needed individual friendship with his parents. He needed their assurance that, "You're all right. You make mistakes, but you have value. You'll amount to something." All that is spoken in the simple, "I want you as a friend."

In their one-on-one role with their child, Mom and Dad model their femaleness and maleness. This is woman, infinitely more complex than any stereotype. This is man.

Again, if this was not the pattern in your family-of-origin, you'll have trouble getting into the swing of treating a teenager as a peer and friend. It's not going to come naturally or spontaneously, but it can be done.

Stop and think for a bit about the male and female roles you grew up with. They weren't seriously contaminated, were they? For example, we counsel families where the woman's only strength, her only ability to manipulate others, lay in being constantly ill and needy. Or the father, a pillar of machismo, never dared demonstrate affection or sorrow. What models did you see in your teen years? Is that what you want your own children to see?

At this time the spouses need each other as a support system, because teens are just plain hard on parents. As teens break away, developing their own identities, the parents have to develop their own identities apart from kids.

"That's ridiculous!" snorts the adult. "Of course I have my own identity."

"Bravo!" we reply. "But we encounter so many people, friends and clients both, who have invested their whole identity —and their self-esteem—in their kids. It's so easy to do. You want the kids to be like you, or better than you, and the family disintegrates. Parents' self image must not depend upon their kids being unrebellious, smart, perfect, or whatever; but so many do."

"True," you say, "but it's not all the parents, especially when the kids go into high school. I may be a famous leader, politician, author, musician, movie star. But at my kid's school I am ever and anon 'So-and-so's mother.' "

"Isn't that the way it is," we agree. That is why good personal boundaries are needed here. And the spouse helps set them.

A final part of working together as a parenting team is to balance privilege against responsibility.

Balance Privilege Against Responsibility

Ruth grew up under circumstances just the opposite of May's. In Ruth's family-of-origin, chaos reigned. Her father was disabled by illness most of her life, and he simply abrogated his position as head of the house to Mom. His health problems kept Mom preoccupied and the family in turmoil. Now Ruth, near the end of the Third Passage of her marriage, faced the adolescence of her daughters aged twelve and seventeen. Ruth had learned early to be her own parent, to be responsible for herself. Now she was compulsive and over-organized, though not militantly so.

The only way Ruth knew to raise teens was the way she had raised herself. She ran their lives. She was never harsh or dictatorial. She was simply always there to do everything for her daughters. She did a lot of their homework. When the twelve-year-old had a falling out with another girl on her soccer team, Ruth talked to the coach, the other parent, and the other girl herself, mending the rift single-handedly. Her daughter received no experience or responsibility in handling even that casual, temporary conflict.

Although the seventeen-year-old was gifted academically, her teachers noted that she never took the initiative on anything. As long as a teacher or coach guided each step, giving her specific orders, she did very well. On any open-ended project, the child sat paralyzed. When teachers voiced complaints, Ruth went to school and talked to those teachers. Her response was to do everything; "I'll supervise her more closely—make sure she gets it done." The teachers realized they were listening to the problem, not the solution, and sent Ruth to our counsel.

Ruth's parents had never presented a model of how to balance privilege with responsibility. Ruth, on her own early, knew complete privilege and complete responsibility beyond her years. She had to learn that lesson of balance now.

Part of Ruth's solution, therefore, was: She had to back off and give her girls autonomy and freedom, including the most important freedom, the freedom to make mistakes. To help her do something she had never seen done or done herself, we gave Ruth some assignments.

One assignment: she was not to supervise the girls' homework. They were to do it or not on their own. Talk about frightening! Ruth sat wild-eyed and weepy as she told us how her daughters' school grades had fallen precipitously. She realized that some evenings the girls were not studying. They weren't always completing assignments or doing required reading. She very nearly stepped in. It took vigorous confrontation from us, and help from her husband. To that point he had been passive, letting the little wife raise the daughters without his interference. The father's passivity was basically a control issue. He invested himself in his job and let that be his sole arena of control. There had been no sharing between Ruth and her husband regarding parenting. They had to learn from the ground up how to be a team.

To begin with, Dad had to step in and tell Ruth, "No. We'll honor what the counselors say and not exert excessive control." As Ruth moved back, her girls gradually assumed some self-responsibility for their schoolwork.

Ruth learned the lesson May and LeRoy came to grasp also: by giving children the freedom to fail, while they are still young and it's safe to do so, that freedom fosters new responsibility rather than breeding irresponsibility.

"James can't handle what I give him now; no way will I give him more freedom and responsibility!" May stormed. As James went through his rebellion, the only response May and LeRoy knew to make was to revoke privileges. Reducing privileges reduced the responsibility to be mature, and that did nothing to bring back into balance that important polarity "Privilege versus responsibility."

In dealing with your child, envision an old fashioned, two-pan balance, the kind of scale blind-folded justice holds aloft. On one side, privilege. In the other pan, responsibility. Add weights to one pan, the other pan requires more weights, too, in order to maintain level balance. "The more I want my child to accept responsibility, the more freedom I must give, appropriately."

You may find this terribly frightening. You must realize that as you grant more freedoms, you are not granting license for irresponsibility. You are laying the foundation for greater responsibility.

You must explain clearly and repeatedly about the balance scale. Your child must understand that to receive more freedom means to take on more responsibility. Fortunately, by early teens, kids can grasp concepts of that sort well.

The most frightening arena of responsibility of all: teen sexuality. May turned white just thinking about James acting out in that area as he acted out in others. "The worst thing I could ever find in his wallet would be a condom," she said, "And it would be the best thing I could find."

May was onto something with that comment, although she had to come to terms with it better. You must also take an immense step with your own child; you must accept and endorse your adolescent's emerging sexuality at the very same time that you are modeling appropriate boundries for sexual expression. After all, God put it there. Denying it isn't going to serve any purpose whatsoever. We suggest that you do this in three healthy ways.

First, you must have accepted your own sexuality.

"Well, of course I do. I mean, I've been married so many years that. . . " May looked confused.

"Are you comfortable with your sexuality?" we asked.

She thought about it a while. "Yes. Yes I am."

"Then that hurdle's past." We know of many cases, however, where Mother thinks sex is nothing more than a duty, or Dad feels sex is dirty. A few people will label all sex as sin, even that within marriage.

Consider one young woman whose mother sat down with her on her wedding day and gave her a long dissertation on sex (the first and only time she'd ever talked about it). It was a duty, certainly no fun, always suspect as being dirty or crude. The daughter married on schedule and got nearly through her Third Passage before it caught up to her. Sex for her had never been good because of both the overt negative message from Mom and the lifetime of hidden messages that had said the same thing. The daughter's crisis came when her own teen daughter entered puberty. Mom had no way to help her own daughter understand that it's okay to be a woman and engage in marital sex. Mom didn't repeat the overt negative messages she herself had heard, but she sent them implicitly. Her daughter lived out the dark side of those negative messages, promiscuously acting out sexually during her early teens. Because the parents had never made internal peace with their own sexuality, the daughter was sexually acting out that unresolved conflict for them.

Second, you must also have completed the sexual dimensions of your prior marriage passages before you can help your children go through this most confusing and frightening physical change of their lives. How did you and your spouse deal with sexuality during your prior years of marriage? Have you built a sexual union? Are you satisfied with your sexual relationship? Have you weeded out and confronted any hidden agendas from your family-of-origin on sexuality? Without positive answers to the above questions, there is no way you and your spouse can be healthy examples to your teen. If there are problems in your marriage's sexual union, the kids will unconsciously pick up on it even if the sexual breakdown is never overtly dicussedin the family. Again, we recommend reading the first two books in our series, *New Love* (Thomas Nelson, 1993) and *Realistic Love* (Thomas Nelson, 1993), if you sense any problems in this arena.

Third, the parents must be certain to recognize, acknowledge, and endorse their teens' sexual feelings. May's eyes got too big to fit in the doorway when we said that. "You can't be serious! James doesn't need one little speck of encouragement to act up. Can you imagine what he'd be doing if I even mentioned something like that? 'Oh boy! Mom says it's okay!' Especially because he only hears what he wants to hear—not what I really say."

We responded, "Pretend you wake up one morning, walk out in the living room and there's an elephant. Full grown elephant. That's impossible! And when everyone else walks around the living room they don't seem to notice it. You think your mind is slipping. How come you're the only one who sees that elephant?"

Teens, boys in particular, wake up one morning with strong sexual feelings and fantasies. This is frightening for a child. Something that suddenly dominates your thoughts—an elephant in your living room—is something no one else will acknowledge. "Am I weird? Doesn't anyone else feel this way? The other guys talk about it all the time, but do they really feel what I feel or are they just saying that stuff to sound good?"

Parents who acknowledge and endorse their children's growing sexual feelings are not encouraging those children to act
them out. To the contrary, a teenager who feels that his or her
sexual needs are heard and validated by Mom and Dad is a teen
who will be much more receptive to hear and respect the parents' moral guidelines. "Banish those thoughts! Get those feelings out of your body!" does nothing to alter the powerful hor-
monal surge of adolescence. The thoughts and feelings stay.

An appropriate response? "I remember when I was your age.
It just about takes you over. It's really hard to keep those feelings in their place until marriage, but it's worth it."

You may have to talk about sex with your teen over and over
again. It can't be said once and then done with. You must be
open and honest and talk frequently with your teens about their
emerging sexuality. And don't use a patronizing tone of voice;
they will immediately pick that up. Be sincere and caring.

Throughout this chapter we've been talking about shoring up
your marriage in relationship to your adolescent. And we've suggested that May and LeRoy Lucas had to take a careful look at
their own relationship too. One of the best ways they could start
was to embrace the intimacy that is possible in this comfortable
passage of marriage.

Chapter 8

Can Your Spouse Fulfill Your Need for Intimacy?

"C ream separators? Oh my, do I remember cream separators!" Lou Ajanian's wife Marj wagged her head. "Every farm had one. Big stainless steel unit that stood on legs in the corner of the kitchen. It was basically a couple of steel tanks, one inside the other. Mom made us girls clean it every day. It broke down into half a dozen parts and you had to scrub and bleach each one to prevent contaminating the next milking. No smell of sour milk, of course. It had to be spotless. Just washing the separator took half an hour. Kids these days have no idea what 'thankless task' means.

"The big dairies separate the milk themselves now, with super-duper equipment. They can separate out the butter cream, and make skimmed milk of any weight they want, better than the old farm separators could. I'm glad for the kids' sake that the old separators are about gone."

There may not be many cream separators in farm kitchens anymore, but numerous separators exist in marriage. Quietly and usually unobserved, they skim off the richness, the good stuff, and leave behind a watery substitute for the real thing. Anyone who grew up on fresh whole milk proclaims how pallid 2 percent is.

By the Third Passage (or frequently even before then), serious threats to intimacy abound. At times they cannot be resolved by a few simple changes or even by writing a new contract. They must be ferreted out and reversed, or the marriage partners will find themselves either stranded at a checkpoint or hopelessly off course.

"When love dies," Debi Newman observes, "it is not in the heat of battle. It's when a partner believes the other will never meet the needs for intimacy."

The seventh task of the Third Passage—Steadfast Love—is to maintain an intimate relationship with your spouse.

The Seventh Task: To Maintain an Intimate Relationship

"But I don't *need* intimacy. Well, yeah. Sex. But not intimacy, not like you're talking about." Lee Atkins, fifteen years a construction superintendent for a major company, sat in our office. His bride of twelve years insisted he undergo counseling or they were finished. So here he was. With his track record at age fifty-one, he didn't really expect this marriage to last forever—this was his third—but he really loved the woman.

"But that's not intimacy. I mean, sex isn't intimacy, right?"

"Sex is only one part of intimacy," we agreed.

"I'm sure some guys need intimacy. And I suppose a little of it's nice. But, well, it's not a requirement for me, like food and water is a requirement, a need. Do you understand what I'm trying to say?"

"We understand clearly. We hear it all the time."

Intimacy is the sharing of the soul—hopes, dreams, fears, shames, joys, sorrows. Intimacy is knowing other people deeply and well and appreciating them anyway. It's an easy, comfortable balance between dependence upon another and independence— the sharing of your life and the living of one's own life; of aloneness and togetherness; of distance and closeness. We talked about interdependence being the opposite of codependence in Chapter 2. True intimacy is interdependence. Early in this passage the marriage relationship is still swinging between the extremes of dependence and independence. By the end of the Third Passage the fine balance can be achieved. Knowing I have a mate for life, I share all, bare all.

Men and women have two needs in their relationships with others, some teachers claim. They need to impact others' lives, and they need to enjoy a personal, intimate relationship. Men tend more toward the need for impact, and women toward relationships, but that's merely a matter of degree. Both have both. An aside: men and women with heightened needs for relationship are going to find themselves especially vulnerable in the public workplace.

If we would convince Lee Atkins that he, like any other man, actually needs genuine intimacy, we would have to show him the barriers to it which he erected within himself. In our counsel, and also in our own lives, we find many barriers to true intimacy.

Root Causes

What are the down-deep barriers to intimacy? See if any of these root causes are spoiling your relationship.

Motives

Theologians call it the sin root: greed, fear, selfishness, an inability to trust, an inability therefore to give and compromise. I want it my way. And I want it all.

Denial

A friend we'll call Jean defended her marriage proudly and vigorously. "We have just about a perfect marriage going," she said. "We've been together twenty years. That says something."

"That's a lot of joy and sorrow, anger and contentment," we agreed.

"Anger? Oh, no. No sorrow. We never hurt each other. That's what I mean when I say we have this perfect marriage."

By looking only at the positives, many couples deny their true feelings. Two persons in the same bed, under the same roof, can't get by without hurting now and then. Masking feelings, denying the speed bumps, is not true intimacy. They are not sharing.

People who look like a perfect couple to the outside world may well be a perfect couple in the privacy of their lives. But they also might be separated from each other even though they're living together—even though they look so good.

Self-preoccupation

Self-preoccupied? What's that? When your interest and attention are focused inwardly, your face is turned away from your
mate. Depression, while it is an illness that deserves much com-
passion, can be another form of self-occupation. The depressed
person is pulled into self-absorption with the pain. Addictions,
similarly, turn the person's attention inward. Even if you hate
yourself, that's still self-centrism. Your attention is on yourself.

Other Preoccupations

"If we had an evening together, it meant the secretaries made
a scheduling error," said Jane Fonda, commenting on her divorce from Tom Hayden. Two busy lives flying in different
orbits can wreck intimacy. Your life doesn't have to be as busy as
a movie star's either. The common pressures and distractions of
modern life suffice.

A formidable barrier looms when both partners work full-time
outside the home because of financial necessity. When the
mother would rather stay home and raise her children herself—
or the father, for that matter—tensions rise just over the situation itself. Romance does not commingle with tension.

Think of all the tugs and pulls. The man, and frequently the
woman also, are under much pressure to be competitive, to suc-
ceed (whatever job success entails). If the man's career has
plateaued, shame, feelings of inadequacy, self-hate or self-disap-
pointment all add to the tension—particularly if his wife's career
is taking off, as it frequently does once the kids get older. Man
and woman both may project such feelings onto each other.
When emotion and stress run rampant, the doors open to an
extra-marital affair.

Then there's just plain physical weariness. There's the pressure
to spend time with the kids, and the load of guilt for not spending enough of it. Neither person has anyone upon which to
dump frustrations; neither one wants to hear the other's problems.

Brian Newman chuckles. "Debi and I solve the problem of
dumping on each other by holing up in opposite ends of the
house. When both of us come off a bad day; and that happens

frequently; we need the separation. We put off decision-making and even face-to-face contact until we're both settled."

By the way, if you've had a bad day at the office, be sure to tell the spouse and kids when you get home. Otherwise, they'll think it's something they've done to put you in such a black mood. Then take the time to be by yourself—relax, exercise, anything to help your mood.

Robert Hemfelt soaks in the hot tub or eats popcorn and watches the news. Susan curls up with country living catalogs and daydreams. Whatever works.

Giving Advice

"But what would my spouse do without my advice?" you protest.

"Depends," we reply. "Did your spouse ask for it, or did you give it unsolicited?" A common example: He shares a problem from work. She volunteers a solution. Her effort comes across as, "You dummy, you couldn't think of this yourself. I have to fix it for you." He was not looking for a solution; he wasn't even complaining, really. He was sharing his problem and his feelings. We find that sometimes this very situation is why one partner stops sharing. Sharing encourages intimacy. Failure to share broadens separation. Fear of criticism or fear of your partner's need to fix it for you stops the sharing.

Feelings

David and Teresa Ferguson, affiliated with the Minirth-Meier, Wilson and Tunnell clinic in Austin, TX, have been through the Third and Fourth Passages of Marriage themselves. Now they work as a team dealing with troubled marriages. They see three negative feelings that cause intimacy to slip away quietly.

The first feeling: I no longer trust you to prioritize me. "We have found," says Teresa, "that after ten years or more of marriage, the husband's priorities usually are: first, his job/career; second, hobbies, TV, or sports; third, his kids; fourth, his wife; and fifth, God.

"His wife's priorities, though, usually rank: first, her kids; second, her church or civic service or her job; third, her husband; fourth, God; and fifth, her own parents."

She's fourth on his list and he's third on hers. That hurts. And

if this priority list is true of your marriage, it is very hard for you
to sustain intimacy.

What's an ideal list? The Fergusons suggest: first, God in my
life; second, my spouse; third, the kids; fourth, job and church;
and fifth, TV, hobbies, or sports. The children are nurtured not
so much by Mom and Dad as by the solid union. Putting the
marriage ahead of the kids as a priority is actually putting the
kids ahead, in the end.

*The second feeling that fosters distance is "I no longer feel you
care because of unhealed hurts."* Picture a cup which holds your
feelings. It's finite. It can only hold so much. Once that cup fills,
something has to go before other things can enter. The person
with untended hurts from childhood, plus an accumulation of
hurts from the marriage itself thus far, has no room left for
feelings of care, love, joy. They get squeezed out by the mass of
pent-up feelings hiding in the cup. The only way to empty the
cup of those feelings, and make room for happier feelings, is to
grieve and release them through the grieving process we've mentioned throughout this book.

*The third feeling stymying intimacy is "I no longer feel your love
since taking has replaced giving."* In the Third Passage, the couple have not really cultivated to this point the art of giving to
each other. Life has been too cluttered until now, what with
career, kids, housing decisions, and all. And, because of accumulated hurts, either partner may fail to recognize when a gift is
being given. With the partnership drifting into complacency,
much is taken for granted. Each partner thinks the other knows
about needs but doesn't care enough to fill them, when in reality, neither partner sees them. Both partners tend to take what
they need by manipulating and demanding.

If these to a greater or lesser extent be the deepest underlying
attitudes in a marriage, the causes and symptoms become all the
more virulent. If you are in the Third Passage, do you see any of
these attitudes and feelings in your own outlook? How about
your partner's?

Symptoms

We look for specific warning signs that repairs are needed, that
the passage has become stuck, unable to mature into the next

stage of life. Does your marriage suffer from any of these common signs of being caught in this passage of marriage?

Sexual Difficulties

If sex ceases or nearly so at this stage of marriage, it does not necessarily mean the marriage is a bad marriage. It does identify that the couple are stuck, hung up in the passage. The sexual paralysis may indicate that deep unresolved hurt, anger, or control issues between the couple exist, and the sexual shut down is a physical and symbolic way of saying two people are out of touch with each other. Sometimes, it indicates that one or both partners have falsely bought into myths about sex and aging and believe that sex tapers off by now (Robert Hemfelt's mother announced to Susan that older people are sexual beings, too; she was in her seventies). Very late in life—beyond the seventies—a couple's love may well transcend the physical, as sexual vigor wanes with age. We're not talking about that here. In this passage, the partners are young enough to comfortably maintain an active and vigorous sex life. If they do not, something wrong is afoot.

We always hesitate to declare a norm as regards to frequency of sexual intimacy, unless you call "extreme variation" a norm. When pressed for a very general ballpark figure, we suggest that two or more weeks between episodes of sexual intimacy and intercourse is a bit too long. Assuming good health in both marriage partners, and assuming no extenuating circumstances (the birth of a baby within the last six weeks, for example), partners in their forties and fifties are probably getting together sexually a couple times a week or more, couples in their thirties somewhat more often.

Trouble signs we look for in counseling are: if sex is less frequent than once a week; if only one partner initiates sex; if one or both partners neglect themselves physically—gain weight drastically, get frumpy, neglect hygiene or such. These are usually barometers that the sex life is deteriorating and therefore the partners are moving apart. Something is going wrong with intimacy.

Charles sought help for sexual impotence. His sexual relationship with his wife had never really been strong in their marriage, and she complained of its infrequency. That in itself is a warning sign: one partner or the other believes frequency is too much or not enough. In recent years, however, "infrequent" trickled away into "non-existent" in Charles's case. Not even his wife bothered to try initiating sex anymore. She had been disappointed too many times.

We insert a disclaimer here: Individual physical or psychological issues may cause impotence or drastically reduced activity. Use of various prescription drugs or alcohol, even short of abuse, can impair performance. Some diseases, such as diabetes, and many kinds of medications (antihistamines, anti-depressants, some heart medicines) hamper performance. Ask your doctor about that when receiving a prescription. A death in the family, extreme anxiety—traumatic events can temporarily cool ardor.

Anger, depression, or fear, which may not be tied to anything in the marriage itself, may generate sexual problems. We know of a man shocked by the sudden loss of his job; things had seemed so secure; the company appeared to be doing well, his job was important. . . and then, out of the blue came the layoff. He'd never been without work in his life before. Devastated, he went through an exasperating six-month period of sexual impotence.

Most frequently, distorted notions or expectations about sex put the clamps on. For instance, when the first baby arrives, Mom or Dad or both gain fifty pounds and let themselves go. Below the conscious level, they are saying, "Sex in a family is wrong. We're now a family. If I'm too fat to be desirable or sexy, we won't have to worry about it." Another example; a woman enters menopause and she or her husband or both falsely believe her sexuality has ended.

When we examine symptoms we look first at the couple's relationship, which may be hindered by hidden agendas or ghosts from their past, but we also cover all the other possible sources, physical as well as others.

Another persistent warning sign is a preoccupation with affairs, either actual or imaginary. When fantasies constantly invade sex, or if one or both spouses prefer fantasy to actual sex, warning bells ring. Charles's wife fantasized sexual unions with persons she knew and also with film celebrities. "As long as you're not doing it," she commented, "it doesn't matter who you're not doing it with. The sky's the limit." Some fantasizing is healthy for eroticism. To obsess, however, is very dangerous and damaging, for this reason. Moments of ecstasy and orgasm are extremely vulnerable bonding times. The partners imprint on each other, in the classic sense. Each time a partner focusses on a person or fantasy other than the spouse, the fantasizer has destroyed the opportunity for powerful bonding that time. That moment is lost. A couple may just get by in Passages One or Two with hit and miss bonding, but by the Third Passage, with its powerful pressure to drift or separate, the couple needs this visceral and emotional bonding to stay together.

We also consider it a warning sign as well as a moral issue if couples rely on pornography to jump-start their flagging sex life. Excessive reliance on masturbation, either gender, as a substitute for marital sex is understandably a big issue as well.

We look, too, for discouragement. By this Third Passage, men find themselves taking longer to achieve and maintain an erection. They may "fold in the middle." The temptation then is to believe the old days are gone forever and just give up. Women produce less lubricant, making penetration, at least in the first moments, more difficult and uncomfortable.

Charles's medical workup showed no physical problems. The hidden emotional agendas we uncovered were the real cause.

Power Struggles

You're unconsciously mad at your spouse for getting paunchy and maybe a little overweight, and otherwise showing signs of aging. You therefore withhold sex as a punishment. That's using sex as a power tool. A woman—or man—who feels otherwise powerless in a relationship may feel sex is the only weapon in her or his impoverished arsenal. Power struggles in other areas of life —the kids, the finances, the degree of interaction with in-laws, autonomy and control in the household—carry over into the bedroom.

Financial Struggles

Charles and his wife did not display this symptom, but many do. Money is a powerful symbol of power and a symbol of the ability to nurture oneself and others. More obvious signs are big debts, bounced checks, bankruptcy. But the signs may be perplexingly subtle. No big warning bells bong, as with bounced checks or unpaid bills. Most frequently, it's simply that they cannot seem to save; they can never get ahead.

Counselors say that the combination house and car payment and all other debts should together total out to less than one-third a couple's take-home pay. Special situations, of course, may well be outside a person's control. In Texas in the eighties, we saw the oil boom collapse. A lot of fortunes caved in with it. However, we also find it a general rule that if a person is prone to repeatedly make speculative deals, that often says something about them emotionally. In some professions, such as the ministry and teaching, the money simply may not be there.

Several years ago we helped a highly driven businessman. It turned out that his hidden agenda was, "The only way to prove I love you is to provide handsomely." As a result he was susceptible to wild investments. He went through several bankruptcies, but he always managed to pull his fortunes back together. In that way he was brilliant. In matters of love, it took us a long time to help him alter his agenda to, "I love you, and I'll do my reasonable best to provide for you." His wife had been on the verge of divorce because she couldn't stand the financial roller coaster ride. They're humming along at a much more modest financial clip now; no steep hills and deep valleys; and he's loving the new, less-hectic lifestyle so much, he's considering retiring. She's all for it.

Another financial warning sign emerges when two partners do not share financial handling and decision making. This need not be a fifty-fifty thing. But both parties should be fully apprised of the union's finances, both having input into decisions, and, ideally, veto power. In distressed marriages, we usually find a significant imbalance in that.

Frequently one partner, usually the husband, deliberately withholds financial information. "If she knows how much we make, she'll just want to spend it." "If she knew the truth, she'd start nagging me to make more." Money and sex are the two big control issues; when they are combined, the mix can be volatile.

Have you ever heard these statements of financial blackmail perpetrated on partners?: "If you loved me you'd buy. . ." Or "I'll cut back your allowance." Or the non-bread winner may say, "I'll spend you into oblivion." Dysfunctional couples may often use money to beat up on each other.

Excessive or Malicious Fighting

Please note: There is nothing wrong with anger and disagreement. In fact, such friction is both necessary and inevitable if persons are to reveal themselves wholly to each other. People in a good marriage argue in fair and appropriate ways. Conflict resolution actually breeds intimacy as we discussed in Chapter 3.

BUT. When fighting is chronic or becomes physical; when it degenerates to physical, verbal or emotional violence and abuse; when it spills over into the kids' arena (either a spouse enlists the kids in a gang effort against the marriage partner, or either spouse takes it out on the kids); when major issues are never resolved; when fights span several days or simmer for long periods; when you find yourself fighting just for the sake of winning; there is a problem.

The subject matter of fights may provide a clue to growing separation. If fighting degenerates into character assassination ("I know you don't love me; you can't love anyone) or taking your partner's comments or actions personally when they weren't meant that way, we look for the deeper problem. When a couple finds themselves fighting about who leaves the toothpaste cap off, the fight is never about toothpaste. It's about unresolved issues both are ignoring. Uncapped toothpaste is easy to see, and it's not painful. Deeper issues, hard to see, almost always hurt, so they are avoided.

Dr. Hemfelt cites the example of a farming couple recently whose wife complained, "After I finally pried him off the sofa, he went out and trimmed the trees in the orchard. He absolutely scalped them!" and she popped photos out of her purse to prove her point. "He did it to get back at me." The trees, of course, were not the issue, and her inappropriate personalization of his actions fit right into the picture. Sometimes it is quite appropriate to see that a partner is getting back in some way. But in many cases, this among them, what the one partner saw as a direct affront was merely the other person's attempt to work off anger in a constructive manner that somehow went awry. The big point is often not the action itself but how the action is perceived.

"Incidentally," says Robert, "Susan claims I scalp our bushes.

A real buzz job. She doesn't take pictures, but she does express pity for the bushes."

We find one other aspect of unfair fighting that warns us of serious separation. One or both persons simply bury anger for a long period. The opposite also counts. One or both partners explode instantly. Even more commonly, we see both happening; the person (or persons) stuffs the anger away until finally, an explosion flings it at the partner all at once.

Physical Separation

In a sense, deliberately separating physically is nearly as painful as divorce. We're not talking here about legal separation, but about more subtle splits. Charles's wife did that. She'd go to the next state to visit Mom for several weeks at a time. Several times a year she'd visit her younger sister for a week or so, just to keep the family bond going. Added up, her little excursions totalled months.

Some separations are necessary, determined by circumstance like a business trip or an illness in the family or military service. Taking the kids to out-of-town events such as contests, medical appointments, athletic games involve separation. But when you separate often for reasons other than that, problems surface. Lonely and angry, and with no other way to get Charles's attention, his wife ruptured the fabric of commitment. We cannot be together, so we will not be together.

Repair

"There was one nice thing about cream separators," Marj admitted. "Filter dolls. Every farm girl had a fancy look-at-it-but-don't-play-with-it doll decorating her bed. It was dressed in milk filters, hundreds of them stitched together in a big frill with colored ribbons and yarn. Out of misery, beauty."

Out of misery, beauty. Improving intimacy will work wonders for a marriage. Philosophers for centuries have delighted to point out how closely akin are love and hate, as if love and hate were two aspects of the same thing. In a large way they are. To the degree you can love a person, to that degree you can also feel strong animosity toward him or her.

"I'll sure buy that!" claimed Lee Atkins. "I was so certain my ex-wife and I would be in love forever. We're talking about deep, deep love here. She hired three different lawyers, each one specializing in a different way to milk the ex. She still can't stand the sight of me, and every now and then she'll call me up and say so. Can you believe it?"

We certainly can. Usually, though, the love-hate tug of war is not that brutal. In most couples it's more mild-mannered, only occasionally getting out of hand. Love is nurtured when our need for impacting others and for enjoying healing, comforting intimacy is well met. Hatred is generated by fear and hurt, and also by the fear of being hurt. Needs have not been met; we fear they never will be. If you remember that love and hate, both of them the most impassioned emotional responses a human being makes, spring from the same roots, you can turn hate around to love, and separation to intimacy.

In the clinic and in private counseling, our patients consider the symptoms to be the most important; after all, they have to suffer with them. We don't ignore the symptoms, but we go beyond them to explore underlying causes. The causes, then, point the way to possible solutions. Treating the symptoms only does no good; the causes will still be there to prevent treatment from "taking" or the causes will generate other symptoms.

Major Damage Control

If you see your marriage in a serious slide toward destruction, you want serious steps to reverse it. Join us as we study further the couple, Rick and Nancy. The process they used employs five steps.

Rick and Nancy, married fifteen years, had daughters aged ten and twelve. They came to us because they could see their marriage and family falling apart and had not the vaguest idea how to snatch happiness out of the brewing disaster. We spoke of some of their problems in Chapter 1. Let's look at their situation in depth now.

Their sex life, we learned, was virtually nonexistent. He considered her cold and unresponsive. She called him emotionally distant, sexually exploitative and mechanical in his lovemaking. They both pursued careers. He tackled his in classic workaholic fashion. She worked as a department store buyer during the day while her girls were in school. We uncovered one of her hidden agendas early: She unconsciously purposed to build enough of a financial cushion that she could leave Rick. The cushion, however, never materialized, because, inspite of dual careers, the marriage had been haunted by unrelenting financial pressure.

Nancy's father, a confirmed womanizer, eventually walked away from his family into the arms of another woman. Rick's father stayed home, but he was hardly closer to his children. Cold and emotionally distant, he pretty much ignored Rick except to explode at him in bouts of rage. Both individuals, therefore, dragged a heavy load of baggage from the past.

To help them unload all that baggage and renew their lives with each other, we led them through five steps toward wholeness. You, too, can use those five steps to help a damaged marriage.

1. *"What is the old family-of-origin wound keeping me away from intimacy?"* Rick and Nancy's were obvious—rage-aholism, neglect, abandonment, distance. You've already explored your own wounds. You, like Rick and Nancy, have to acknowledge them. Rick and Nancy had not, not in their early years of marriage, not recently. Both buried the old pain. That put deep cracks in the foundation of their union. One way they un-buried them was to hear each other's story.

Previously, they constantly attacked each other for not sharing, for failing to be part of each other's world.

"He doesn't care about my interests."

"She doesn't listen and doesn't give a hang."

That all stopped as we had each one tell the other what it was like to grow up in that family-of-origin. They ceased the litany of mutual blame as they heard from each other the pain of growing up. The tone of the session shifted dramatically. Each person felt more sensitive and compassionate. Each became a better listener.

2. *"What are the wounds in my own marriage now that steer me away from intimacy?"* Review the earlier wounds of your own marriage. How did your spouse hurt you? We hope they are not as extreme as Rick and Nancy's. Nancy began to suffer from a chronic bleeding stomach ulcer in her mid-thirties. Rick didn't really mean to seem indifferent, but the situation frightened him. He felt confused, uncertain. What should he say, if anything?

What should he do? He had no idea how to deal with it all; he ended up simply withdrawing out of fear. Nancy, understandably, felt abandoned. In our office she talked about the pain of the occasion when she went for one of her crucial follow-up tests to determine if surgery would be necessary.

"I begged him to go along," she related. "He sort of agreed. Then he simply 'forgot.' He just didn't show up at the hospital."

"I got snowed under at the office. Even if I had remembered, I wouldn't have been able to get away," Rick complained.

"Oh, no! You could call the shots, Rick. You're the manager. It was you. Not circumstance. I was devastated. I don't know how I got through it alone. And believe me, I had to walk that whole road alone."

Rick and Nancy both had to grieve out the fear and anger generated by prior disappointments and letdowns. It was the only way to clear away the wreckage of the past.

You, too, must similarly clear away such wreckage. You will find that some of that painful wreckage is due to false assumptions. And that is the next step:

3. *"What assumptions have I made about how my spouse sees me?"* Nancy assumed, because of his distance and withdrawal, that Rick didn't care. She assumed he was insensitive to pain and the threat to her health. Maybe he didn't love her as much as she had supposed; maybe he didn't love her at all. In reality, he was feeling intense fear, not indifference, but culture and his early life with an undemonstrative father had conditioned him to hide it. He had never given himself permission to talk about feelings, certainly not to talk about or admit fear.

If by this Third Passage your needs are not being met, you will start to make negative assumptions about what your spouse feels. Those assumptions, apart from being unjust, destroy intimacy. Sometimes the assumptions are true or at least border on truth. The vast majority are not.

Rick, meanwhile, was assuming that because of Nancy's bout with an ulcer, she was no longer as interested in physical love. She took his distance to mean that he saw her as damaged merchandise. Can a vicious cycle of assumptions and counter-assumptions be operating in your marriage? Have you two ever simply sat down and talked about what you feel and what you think each other feels? It may come as a vivid revelation that what you think you know about your spouse simply is not true.

Questions 1, 2, and 3 adressed inhibitions and false assumptions that keep the healthiest of couples separated. With questions 4 and 5, we ask couples to explore how they can move back together.

4. *"What fears and resentments do I harbor that my spouse won't reciprocate my efforts?"* we ask couples to ask each other. "Would you make the time and effort to step into your spouse's world?"

"Well, sure, I suppose. But you don't understand," Nancy insisted. "He wouldn't return that to me."

"Have you asked him?"

"It's not that easy. You see," Nancy said, "we're so different. He likes futuristic and science-fiction movies; that boring high tech type stuff. I like romantic movies. He only likes go-go-go business travel; I want to take a cruise or something else leisurely. He would spend his whole life puttering around in the backyard. I'd like to buy a vacation home somewhere, but he's never been willing to spend money on a home away from home."

Rick picked it up. "Our differences are too extreme to patch. I appreciate formal worship. She wants to go to this casual folk service. We end up in two cars on Sunday morning. She goes to these art lectures all the time. I hate them. Politics; you name it. We're on opposite sides of the fence."

Both persons feared that any effort they made to enter their partner's world would go unreciprocated. This is nothing more than the old primal human fear of abandonment or rejection, concealed in very cloudy dress. Both Rick and Nancy had to ventilate that fear by voicing it. They had to sit down and discuss it back and forth. Once on the table, it can be dealt with.

5. *"What am I willing to give in order to get?"* Liken this final step to a cultural exchange program. We send a student abroad and the host country sends a student over here. In the process we export Americanism and improved understanding, and bring the customs and traditions of another culture into our home. If a married couple have drifted off into separate worlds, freezing intimacy, they must rejoin, reconnect, reunite. They have to essentially learn a foreign culture—the life of their spouse.

Rick and Nancy sat down for a round of business-like negotiating. "If you do such and so, I'll do so and so." As cold and mechanistic as it was, it got the attitude of sharing back in place again. As you tackle your give and take, remember that it works only if the other steps are completed first.

You complain, "I shouldn't have to go through mechanical steps to do that." We agree. But many couples need that mechanical bargaining because they have become strangers. They have forgotten how to share. They are suspicious, cautious, uncertain of each other's motives. They must relearn the needs, tastes, interests, and passions of their spouse. It's very much like two people visiting faraway lands and getting to know each other.

Rick and Nancy hit a hard bump in this step. They agreed to work past that fear of rejection. They agreed to step into each other's worlds on a give-and-take basis. That's how Rick ended up on the South Texas coast over the Memorial Day weekend looking at a possible beach home for purchase. He despised bugs. May is a buggy time of year. He didn't like sand. There he was out there in the bright sun looking at prospective vacation homes he thought they could ill-afford. "If it means that much to you," he said, "I'll try." He spent the day marching in and out of beach bungalows that only symbolized to him an unnecessary diversion from his workaholism. But he was there, contributing his "what I'm willing to give in order to get." That's what counted.

Back in the peace and orderliness of their suburban home at last, with no sea gulls dive bombing them, Rick invited Nancy to a science fiction film series at the local college—"Building the Future Is Now" was its title. Nancy declined.

And right there, the whole intimacy-building project went somewhere in a handbasket. Rick was furious. He went way way, way out of his way for her and she couldn't spend one lo' evening at a futuristic film series he was sure she would immensely interesting. His fury wasn't all just anger, you was actually that old nagging fear that she would abandor his efforts, fail to join his world, leave him holding the ? could not consciously recognize or verbalize these fear were there fuelling his anger. Nancy apologized, as crass error was pointed out to her. They cautiou' tantly started over with the sixth task. The second time, it worked. They were committed somehow, someway to join one another's worlds. It wouldn't be easy.

Sampling each other's world does more than just build intimacy, although that is its primary purpose. Rick and Nancy's diversity was not a barrier in their lives, but a wonderful source of enrichment. By sharing in each other's pleasures they could tap into that enrichment. Your diversity is just as rich. And, your marriage is more valuable as your intimacy is rebuilt. This is the ultimate fruit of this Third Passage.

Chapter 9

Have You Completed the Third Passage?

Everyone seated at the conference table in the Minirth-Meier Clinic in Richardson, Texas, had been married at least ten years. Many were nearer the twenty-year mark. Rick and Nancy were among them.

Dr. Hemfelt passed around eleven legal-sized pads, one to each person. "I'll give you eight categories," he explained. "For each of them, think about the dreams and expectations you started out with in your marriage. Whether they were exaggerations or illusions you harbored, or seem quaint or nonsensical now, write them down. Then write down a brief description of what you see as the reality. How do you view those dreams now? Have you abandoned them? Did you achieve them? Take what time you need."

This exercise can be conducted in a couples group. You can do it yourself at home. Its purpose is to clarify the issues of your marriage, and how realistically you see its future. This then becomes a good guide as to how well you are completing this passage. It also provides an insight into what you might want to change.

Balancing the Dream with Reality

We invite you to explore your past and present and thereby perhaps see your future. Do this by running down through the following exercises. When Rick and Nancy participated in this activity, they provided answers we typically hear from couples over and over. As you go through these statements, try to look at both the positives and negatives of your own reality.

1. Sexual romance

When Nancy filled in her dreams in this area, she listed the following: *"I assumed romance would be similar to what I read in romance novels, continually intense and passionate."* Now list your own specific dreams on sexual romance below:

_____

_____

_____

Write a description of your marriage as it is now (For instance: *"We have had a good relationship. It fulfills me if I reign in my original dream"*):

_____

_____

_____

Rick had this to say about his vision of his marriage now: *"I guess it's a convenient arrangement. But not too exciting. The passion has been zero for a long time."*

2. Finances

List your dreams in this arena. Rick's were: *"I had planned to own my own business by this time and to be making enough money for Nancy to be home full-time with the girls."* What are yours:

_____

_____

Now reality. Rick's reality was: *"I'm an area manager for someone else. But at least the job is secure even though our per-*

sonal finances always seem to be out of bounds." What's your financial reality? _____

_____

3. Social prestige

List your aspirations in this area. Nancy put down the following: *"I grew up on Bon Aire Drive. My parents were top of the pile. I expected to be there when we moved here."* What are your aspirations:

_____

_____

In reality, Nancy said: *"We've never attained social prominence in this new town and we never will. On the other hand, the girls are in good schools. Rick and I both have well-paying jobs. This community seems to be a good place to raise a family."* What's your reality?

_____

_____

_____

4. Sharing with friends

Rick's dreams were: *"I'm gregarious and outgoing by nature, so I pictured my wife and me with a wide circle of ten or fifteen close couples, and we'd entertain every weekend."* What are your dreams?

_____

_____

_____

The reality of Rick's social life: *"I find it hard to accept that we've got maybe two or three close couples we socialize with. There's not a lot of close sharing, and my wife is the opposite; she doesn't like to entertain. Frankly, I don't see anything positive here."* Your social reality?

_____

_____

_____

5. Dream of children

This category has two parts. One is whether you wanted children and if so, how your reality matches with the dream. Nancy's dream: *"I always wanted to have two children—a girl and a boy. The boy first, then the girl."* What were your dreams of children?

_____

_____

The reality. Another couple in Dr. Hemfelt's group put down the following: *"One of four couples struggle with infertility and we're one of them. We've tried everything. My husband is resigned to the fact we won't have biological children, but I'm having trouble with it. So I guess you'd say we're halfway; he's there but I'm not."* Nancy's reality was: *"I did get two children. Both girls and am I glad for them, but I have to be honest and say that I'm still missing the boy we never had."* What are your realities with children?

_____

_____

The second part of this category has to do with how your children are turning out. Does that approach the original dream? Rick's dream: *"I always wanted my children to excel in academics."* What were your dreams for how your children should turn out?

_____

_____

The reality of Rick's kids: *"My daughters are average students. They had some problems during their early school years, but they seem to be learning adequately now."* Your reality on your children's growth and development?

_____

_____

6. *Spiritual*

What are your dreams in this area? A woman in Dr. Hemfelt's group listed the following: *"While I was growing up, my family was constantly involved in church, all of us. We loved it and it was a vigorous church."* List your spiritual dreams:

_____

_____

_____

This woman's reality was: *"My husband is a good man, and a Christian. He's saved. We go to church every week, but it's not the center of our lives. I had to accept that those growing-up days are probably gone forever and I can't replicate what I grew up in. It's not just my husband. I can't find a church around here as vibrant as my old home church."* What are your spiritual realities?

_____

_____

_____

7. *Miscellaneous dreams*

By miscellaneous we mean that sort of dream—or dreams— that might begin, "Someday I'd like to _____," or "When I'm married I want us to _____ whatever." Dreams that are unique to you and don't fall into any other category. Nancy's were: *"I always dreamed I'd somehow be able to enjoy lots of world travel and that we would own a vacation home out of state. My parents did that in their younger years, but not after I was born."* List any other dreams you can think of below:

_____

_____

_____

Now, good old reality, Nancy's reality: *" Rick and I are so busy with our jobs and the kids' activities, we barely have enough time to take a family vacation each year. We are looking at vacation homes, but that dream is probably a long way off. Now I look forward to just making it to the beach every now and then for a long weekend. Any international travel is way in the future, if at all. I have replaced my dream of international travel with an insatiable interest in geography. I subscribe to* National Geographic. *I go to every travel program or foreign lecture that I hear about. I spend lots of time at the library in the geography section. It's not the same thing, but it's a taste of all those far-away places with strange-sounding names."* Now list your realities and how they may or may not be compensating for any unrealized dreams you mentioned above:

_____

_____

_____

8. *My spouse in general*

Rick's dreams (and Nancy cringed when she heard them): *"What can I say? To be honest, she was going to be built like a* Sports Illustrated *swimsuit model, earn a Ph.D., and cook like Julia Child."* Be honest, what were your dreams of your marriage partner?

_____

_____

His reality that he had to face and appreciate: *"Would you believe an AA at a junior college? No swimsuit model, but she's healthy now. She was very sick and that scared me to death. And man, can she cook! I'm starting to see how lucky I am."* Your reality in your spouse:

_____

_____

Those glaring deficits, where reality comes nowhere near matching your dreams and aspirations, must be grieved through. Remember the grieving process we mentioned in Chapter 4? If you have unfulfilled dreams, you must grieve their loss. When your dream and reality match or nearly so, you've ample cause to celebrate. Celebration is the other side of the grief coin and is totally appropriate. If none of your realities come close to fulfilling your original aspirations, look again at that area. Did you set your dreams too high? That, too, should be grieved.

This little exercise prepared Rick and Nancy and the rest of their group for the following introspection—how had their marriage progressed to date and what could they do to improve it?

How Well Have You Survived the Third Passage?

If you feel your marriage has progressed along sufficiently in years or maturity to pass from the Third Passage into the Fourth, we invite you to take the following quiz. Xerox a copy for your spouse. Over the next few weeks both of you fill out the questions separately. Then plan a special date to discuss your results.

Drs. Deborah and Brian Newman use these simple questions to rate their clients' progress. As the Newmans do, if you see an area that needs adjustment, work on it. Conversely, if you both completed a task successfully, celebrate it.

Each set of questions is organized under the specific tasks we discussed throughout this book. Rick and Nancy were given this assignment to complete over the next month. They set a future time to discuss their results with their counselor.

Even though they weren't passing into the Fourth Passage yet (they had been married only fifteen years), this quiz showed them what needed work before they reached the point of the next passage. Likewise, if your marriage is still immersed in the Third Passage, use the following questions as guideposts to target areas you and your spouse need to emphasize in the next few years before you enter the Fourth Passage of Renewing Love.

Task One: Maintain An Individual Identity Along with the Marriage Identity

A goal of this passage from the first has been to maintain and develop your own identity, lest your uniqueness be smothered in the comfort and complacency of your marriage. Reworded, you must avoid a codependent relationship with your spouse in which you become either buried in enmeshment, or estranged in constant conflict.

Again, we offer an exercise to help you think about this. Weigh your situation with these statements. Do they pertain to you? How well have you established an identity of your own apart from your marital identity?

Rick and Nancy had slid far down on the independent side of the codependency wheel we discussed in Chapter 2. Their marriage had turned into an enmeshment of constant conflict. Both were fiercely independent and wrapped up in their own worlds and interests. They had a long climb to get back to the top of the wheel. The following exercises helped them see how to do that.

Nancy and Rick had no problem filling in how many friends they had individually. As a matter of fact, they both managed to foster many friendships with others. It was with each other and as a couple that this area lacked.

How About You?

"I can name three friends with whom I'd like to spend the day. I can trust them with most (but not all) secrets."

1. _____
2. _____
3. _____

Early in their marriage, Nancy had many fantasies about spending time with Rick together. She secretly wanted to take a cruise together for their tenth anniversary. But as time went on, kids came, the jobs picked up, the tenth came and went—no special occasion or reason for celebration. She started dreaming of taking vacations alone—the international travel she always coveted. When pressed, she finally filled in the following thing she could plan to do with Rick:

"A honeymoon alone for a weekend at the coast."

Rick suggested that Nancy come with him on some of his business trips. It was a compromise. Business and travel combined. But it was a means of generating some togetherness.

"I can picture several things my spouse and I can do together in the next ten years. At least one of those things is more my idea than my spouse's."

1. _____
2. _____
3. _____

Now look over the following statements. Check those that apply to you. Each of them is designed to see how much of an individual identity you have been able to build or keep within your union. They also measure whether you've managed to build a marriage identity—a union based on interdependence, not independence or codependence.

_____ My marriage/family role (husband/wife, mother/father) doesn't completely define who I am and is not my only purpose for living.

_____ One of the ways my spouse encourages me is to be my own person and to pursue my individual dreams.

_____ My mate is one of my best friends.

_____ I consider myself to be a multifaceted person. I have many interests that don't exclusively include my role in the family and my marriage.

_____ I feel the freedom in my marriage to grow as a person; my husband/wife doesn't try to make me fit into a certain mold.

_____ I value my spouse's opinions and feel he/she values mine.

_____ I have pursued interests my mate advised against, but he/she has been supportive even if it lead to a mistake. (He/She never says "I told you so.")

_____ I can list at least seven characteristics about myself to describe who I am:

1. _____
2. _____
3. _____
4. _____
5. _____
6. _____
7. _____

Our shared marriage identity has grown and changed through the years in the following positive ways:

_____ It doesn't totally devastate my spouse if I do things that are out of character for me.

_____ My partner is a person who knows all about me, but invites me to grow as a person.

_____ My spouse and I share a sense of unity. If the world gets too much for one of us, we know the other is going to be there.

_____ I consider my marriage to be an anchor in the storms of life, in spite of the fact some of the storms are coming from our conflict.

Rick and Nancy could check some of these but not others. It became glaringly obvious to them that they had both managed to build individual personal identities well. Nancy's self-worth was not tied up in her daughters or her role as Rick's wife. Neither was Rick's identity tied to Nancy's. But their independence had managed to flame their conflicts and put them in a tenuous, emotional situation. They had not built a marriage identity. And, they both came to realize that was what they wanted and needed.

If you weren't able to check most of these statements, you may not have built a steadfast marriage and personal identity yet. A closer watch of your position on the codependency wheel may be warranted.

Task Two: Say the Good-byes

Without saying good-bye, you cannot say hello. You must hang up the phone before you can make another call. You must leave behind the past to enjoy the present and look forward to the future. Without saying good-bye, you cannot go on to the next passage. How well have you done this? Check the following statements to see.

_____ I believe I have said good-bye to my ideal parent and have come to terms with the reality of who they are and who I have become.

_____ I have done all I can do to come to a peaceful relationship with my parents or with the memory of my parents.

_____ I have come to terms with my childhood.

_____ I have a strong relationship with God to help me through the crises of life.

_____ I realize that nothing is foolproof. No one has ultimate power or security other than God.

_____ I consider God to be the CEO of our marriage.

_____ Our spiritual orientation is a strength of our marriage.

_____ I can depend on my spouse to help me get through the crises of life and he/she can depend on me to do the same.

_____ So far, the crises we have faced have helped us grow closer as a couple.

_____ I am not afraid to reach out for help when the crises seem too much.

_____ I have realized some of the unrealistic demands I've put on my spouse (expecting he/she to be a certain way). I have grown to accept my partner more deeply and realistically.

_____ I don't feel trapped in my marriage.

Nancy could not check many of these statements. Rick had, in her eyes, abandoned her during her time of crises (her bouts with a recurrent ulcer and the threat of surgery). This emotional wound cut wide and deep. It would take *a lot* of time and patience to heal it. Both of them had managed to say good-bye to their parents as the ideal parents and to their childhood issues with our help. They could now focus on the job at hand—the state of their marriage in the present. Fortunately, they both realized that God was the pillar of their union—they had this "head knowledge," but they had to practice it in their hearts and souls.

Task Three: Overcome the Now-or-Never Syndrome

Nancy succumbed to this temptation of the Third Passage; she secretly planned to leave Rick when she was financially able. She wanted to do it while she still had a chance to find someone else. She was shocked at how little of the following statements she could check. How about you?

_____ I know firsthand the reality of the question "What's it all been about so far?" and I have adequately grieved through and accepted the pain of those doubts.

_____ I understand that there may be an urge to follow some unhealthy roads to deal with this reality and I have a good support group to keep me from taking any of them.

_____ I have made a new commitment to stay in my marriage no matter what it takes.

_____ I have a list of dreams and need to prioritize the unrealized ones and work toward the ones that are complimentary to my spiritual walk and identity.

_____ I see my marriage as a tremendous investment and want to enjoy the multitude of dividends to come.

_____ My marriage is a priority in my life, falling only behind my relationship with God.

_____ I can list at least ten positive qualities about my spouse:

1. _____

2. _____

3. _____

4. _____

5. _____

6. _____

7. _____

8. _____

9. _____

10. _____

_____ I have dealt with the disenchanted feelings I have about my spouse.

_____ I can honestly say that I respect my partner.

_____ I have learned to appreciate one thing about my mate that seemed only a weakness in our early years of marriage.

_____ In our marriage, we are able to talk with each other about personality traits that need improving. We are able to do this in a way that leads to growth in each other.

_____ I have grieved the fact that I didn't marry Cinderella or Prince Charming after all, and I know that there is no one more perfect for me.

How well have you overcome the now-or-never syndrome? If you couldn't check most of these statements, you are probably harboring a feeling of desperation about your marriage. If so, are you looking for ways to get out of it, emotionally or physically?

As part of their healing process, Rick promised to take Nancy on a wonderful exotic vacation abroad for their twentieth anniversary. He wanted to help her realize one of her unmet dreams. She wouldn't believe him, though, until he set up a special bank account just to save for that trip. Then she could get excited about all the researching and planning.

Task Four: Practice True Forgiveness

For Nancy, this task was especially hard. Rick's abandonment during her battle with the ulcer was more painful than the prospect of surgery itself. She held a bitter grudge against him. We helped her realize that this grudge was hurting her more than Rick. How about you? Can you practice true forgiveness? Check the following to see.

_____ My spouse is not an unforgivable person.

_____ At times I have a great deal of anger towards my partner, but for the most part, I love him/her.

_____ Sometimes it is only by the love of God that I can forgive my spouse, but I do it.

_____ I don't hold onto the past hurts in my marriage.

_____ I don't bring up the past in current arguments with my mate.

_____ Both of us have hurt the other. Forgiveness is a daily need in our marriage, and we attempt to practice that forgiveness on a daily basis.

_____ I feel my spouse has completely forgiven me.

_____ I have learned more about the depth of God's love by forgiving my partner and loving him/her.

_____ I believe forgiveness is essential to my marriage's health.

_____ I have been willing to forgive even when I don't feel like forgiving.

_____ I understand that forgiveness is an ongoing process.

_____ I understand I must make a conscious decision to forgive, I can't wait until I feel like forgiving.

_____ I realize that by forgiving I am _not_ being revictimized. I am merely forgiving the person, not the act.

_____ I have set necessary boundaries in my marriage to prevent future offense. These boundaries give me added strength to practice forgiveness for the past.

You can gauge the amount of unresolved anger and resentment you hold against your spouse by how little of the statements you could check. Nancy found enormous relief when she was finally able to forgive Rick.

"I forgive you, Rick. I don't understand what you did and I don't like it, but I truly forgive you. And, I love you." Tears filled Nancy's eyes as she looked up at her husband. Inside, a feeling of comfort spread—a weight lifted off her heart.

She saw Rick's eyelids quiver and his eyes swim in tears. *I can't remember ever seeing Rick cry,* Nancy thought. They embraced.

It took awhile, but when Nancy sincerely forgave Rick, she felt immensely better. Only then was she open to accepting him again as her lover and nurturer.

Task Five: Accept the Inevitable Losses

There are few absolutes in our world: one is you will ultimately age and die. A very real loss in this Third Passage is your youth. Approaching middle age with dignity and enthusiasm takes some real willpower. See how well you're doing this by checking the appropriate statements below if they apply to you.

_____ I recognize the degree of losses that result from entering mid-life, and I'm not afraid of them.

_____ I've been able to say good-bye to my lost youth.

_____ I've noticed some changes in my body.

_____ I'm not afraid of growing older.

_____ I can list at least seven positive things about my aging.

1. _____
2. _____
3. _____
4. _____
5. _____
6. _____
7. _____

_____ I can list at least seven positive things about my mate's aging.

1. _____
2. _____
3. _____
4. _____
5. _____
6. _____
7. _____

_____ I have grieved my lost youth and unrealized dreams.

_____ I have surveyed my financial dreams and have come to terms with how to live with or without them.

_____ I'm either in the grieving process or in the resolution process of all the inevitable losses in my life to this point.

By how little statements he could check, Rick found that he was really afraid of growing old. His body was not as trim and firm as it used to be. He worked out furiously at the club trying to keep himself fit and he was—for his age. But he had to accept he was never going to achieve the physique of a man in his twenties or thirties.

Interestingly enough, when Rick and Nancy started working on their marriage, their sex life improved. Nancy found him physically desirable and told him so over and over. "So much for needing a great bod!" he said. His sexual performance improved when he accepted his aging as a natural process. "A little experience goes a long way," he commented with a wink.

But, Rick also had to grieve the loss of his financial dream. At his stage of life, he wasn't interested in quitting a prominent job to start his own business. It was an unfulfilled career dream that he had to grieve and accept.

Task Six: Help Your Adolescent Become an Individual

Rick and Nancy were just beginning to feel the effects of this task. Darla, their twelve-year old, was entering middle school. Next year she would be a teenager. She was a good enough kid. She followed the rules, did her schoolwork, helped Mom around the house. But Dianne, their ten-year old, now there was a problem. She acted like a teenager at eight. She was a constant source of conflict between Nancy and Rick. They disagreed fervently on her discipline. "Why can't you be more like your sister?" they said to her. As they perused the following statements and with our help, they found that forewarned is forearmed. As their marriage improved so did their children's behavior. Check the following statements to see what shape your parenting arsenal is in:

_____ I can attest that adolescence is an age of pandemonium.

_____ Our children don't come between my wife/husband and me.

_____ Our children feel pretty secure that we are not headed for the divorce court.

_____ When we disagree about how to handle our children, we talk about it and come to some kind of conclusion and united position.

_____ We have special couple-time apart from family-time.

_____ We are available to our children to help them weather the storms of growing up.

_____ We pray together for wisdom on how to raise our children.

_____ When one of us gets frustrated with our kids, the other always is there to lean on and take up the slack.

_____ We don't use the children to get back at each other.

_____ We can share our pain, guilt, and frustration over our children with each other.

_____ We are preparing to let our children grow up and grow away from us.

_____ We agree on how to raise our children.

_____ I understand that our children need to feel secure by living within a strong marriage.

Look back over your responses. How about your spouse's? Did these statements bring up any issues needing discussion, introspection? Kids, especially teens, will pick up on uncertain parents. If you couldn't answer most of the statements in the affirmative, you may need some strengthening in your parenting arsenal.

Task Seven: Maintain an Intimate Relationship

More than any other task, this one posed the most problems for Rick and Nancy. Their marriage had suffered long years of neglect and abuse. Each of the following statements provided a starting point for them to see where they could begin to rebuild the foundation of a lasting union between them:

_____ I know the deepest hurt my spouse has felt in the last year.

_____ My partner and I have time alone together on a regular basis.

_____ My mate is the one person closest to me. He/she knows my innermost feelings.

_____ There really isn't anything that I can't tell my spouse.

_____ I look forward to seeing my partner at the end of each day.

_____ We maintain an intimate sexual relationship that is satisfying to both of us.

_____ Our fights and disagreements regularly reach a place of resolution that is satisfying to both of us.

_____ We work together when it comes to family decisions and issues.

_____ I would not describe our fighting as excessive or malicious.

_____ It isn't unusual for one of us to surprise the other with a special evening out.

_____ I like to think of growing old with my spouse.

If you or your spouse couldn't check most if not all of these statements, intimacy may be wanting in your marriage. Frankly, we'd be surprised if you did check all the statements. Intimacy is the single most difficult emotion to keep alive as a marriage grows old. Celebrate those areas where you have managed to keep intimacy and romance alive. Work harder on the others that need intimacy-building.

Lagniappe

Susan Hemfelt sits at her kitchen table, her coffee mug at her side, and through the glass double door watches her children playing in the yard. "There are a number of things Robert and I do that aren't exactly essential to a healthy marriage. They're treats. Dessert, you might say. Lagniappe.

"You can't follow a cookbook list of items and expect a perfect marriage. But there are fun things you can do to make a good marriage better, and help yourself survive the daily grind."

Here is Susan's list, with some of her comments in places. Some of the items you may be able to use as is. Some of them you may wish to adapt to your particular circumstance. Some of them, economics and scheduling logistics simply will not permit.

_____ Take, at least, a one-week vacation without the kids. ("Okay, maybe two days. I guess we ought to be realistic.")

_____ Carve out some time weekly to be alone together as a couple, other than bedtime. ("Not a movie. Interact.")

_____ Buy a spiral notebook and list all the positive aspects and accommplishments of your years together. ("Get ridiculous. Be serious. And absolutely no negatives.")

_____ Have your picture made as a couple and display it somewhere.

_____ Issue genuine compliments to your spouse. Don't let your mate take it for granted that you noticed.

_____ This is a good time to review retirement goals and plans.

_____ While you're at it, review funeral arrangements and living wills.

_____ Be sure each has a separate hobby and participates in it at least once a week.

_____ In that notebook, list the positive points of crises in your marriage. ("Sure there are some. There are always some. You might even get a laugh out of it; or out of your efforts to find something.")

_____ Plan activities to do with other couples at least once a month without kids.

_____ Assess your church participation. Be active. ("But assessment means looking to keep a balance too. Consider if you are participating at the expense of your family time together.")

A New Contract

"I envy counselors and psychiatrists," Rick confided on one occasion. "They understand people. They don't have these problems like Nancy and I have, with communication going bust and all."

The envy is misplaced. Robert and Susan, Frank and Mary Alice, Brian and Debi—four of whom are professionals who work daily with the marriage problems of others—still have to work through problems of their own. Every couple, no matter how well trained or how poorly prepared, must face the challenges of marriage on a very personal basis. No one is exempt.

And that's good, because that means everyone can also reap the rewards: a sense of individuality within the togetherness; a healthy interdependence within the relationship; a high level of intimacy; the freedom to be oneself which supplants any fear of loss in the relationship. The marital roles change as the situation dictates, but the foundation of the marriage remains undisturbed. The walls can be moved and another story added on, but the foundation bears the weight.

Rick and Nancy found, after months of effort, their marriage was worth saving. Once all the mud and dirt had been scratched off, they found a shining jewel at the root of their relationship. They looked forward to navigating the rest of the Third Passage. And, they found it necessary to restate their reasons for being married.

Chapter 10

The New Contract

"**W**hy write a new reason to be married now?" scoffs the skeptic. "If I didn't already have a reason, do you think I'd be married this long?"

One of our patients had a reason: She couldn't think of any good excuse to divorce. That was a fragile reason. We've heard other, more valid reasons, like the many Christians who believe the Bible verse, "God hates divorce," and therefore are committed to remain married. We suggest that you carefully consider the covenant agreement between your spouse and yourself. It should be a key part of your renewed contract.

"I guess we need to write a new marriage contract because we blew our old one," Rick said.

"Not really," Dr. Hemfelt answered. "You and Nancy need to write a new marriage contract because you both have changed so much. Your needs and outlooks are different now than they were fifteen years ago."

After all Rick and Nancy had learned, grieved, and resolved together, it was time to rediscover and reaffirm the new ways they felt about each other. What better way to do this than in writing.

Therapists recommend journaling to their clients on a regular basis. Putting something in writing is not only therapeutic it is also practical. A person is more apt to understand and see his/ her thoughts clearly if they have been pulled out of their brain away from all the other mumbo-jumbo and put on paper concretely.

Concrete also defines what a written contract does. Somehow if the commitment is put in writing, it is more valid. It is concrete. And like concrete, it is less likely to be broken. The renewed marriage commitment is a reflection of new realities as well as old promises. It is not the covenant promise itself, but the working guide to that promise.

What might a new (or renewed, if you wish) marriage contract entail? Dr. Hemfelt discussed this with the group. "The contract should contain restated commitments to each other, to the marriage, and to God." he explained.

"Can you be more specific?" Nancy asked.

"Sure, let's go over what you might want to put in a contract." Dr. Hemfelt answered. "I suggest beginning with a commitment to each other. You're the parties of the contract. So start there."

"How do we do that?" Nancy asked. "Just say 'I commit to you for life.' I don't know if I can say that honestly."

"No, honesty must be the hallmark of the contract," Dr. Hemfelt explained. "While the goal is to reach a position where both partners can reaffirm a lifelong commitment, you may have to take small steps toward that goal. In a distressed marriage, one may only be able to affirm at first, 'I am committed to be in the marriage for the present, and I am open to work on our major difficulties. I hope and pray that at some future point that commitment can become rock solid.'

"Prior to making this commitment in writing, you must explore what that commitment means."

"Pardon?" one of the men in the group asked.

"Look over the following items. Each of them make up a part of the commitments I mentioned." Dr. Hemfelt passed out a xeroxed page to each of them. "I'll read these over with you as a group. Then, I suggest you go home and discuss them with your spouse."

How About You?

Discuss the following items with your mate. They serve as a basis for any committing statements you will make to each other as part of your renewed marriage contract.

_____ "We renew our original pledge of fidelity."

To guard against the remote chance of straying, as part of your new contract you may want to mutually agree to avoid any and all flirtations, suggestive comments, and careless touching with the opposite sex, tempting situations—in short, any first step down the wrong road. Don't deny the sexual energy between men and women ("Aw, I don't have to worry about that. I'm fat and forty-five") that is always there.

_____ "We each promise to keep the union strong."

We see a lot of ambivalence in this passage. You love and hate the life you have now. In your contract, train that ambivalence into a firm decision to stay with your mate and to love that person. Note those are two different decisions.

_____ "We'll each find a same-sex soulmate."

An executive who found himself in an extra-marital affair and was later restored back to his wife says: "I would encourage every man to have another man he can look eyeball to eyeball with and talk about tough issues of life; to be accountable to. Every man needs that kind of friend." This should not be a parent or sibling (they're too close, and share too many of your own anomalies). You might want to write a friend into your contract. Women should have a woman friend too.

_____ "We commit to the spiritual growth possible now."

You are at last capable of putting away the persons (Mom and Dad particularly), things, and institutions that could function as gods in your life and seek out God Himself in a new dimension. The commitment to spiritual growth means periodically reviewing your life. Are some of those non-gods creeping back into it, like:

_____ Success on the job?
_____ The biggest (or cleanest) house on the block?
_____ The fastest boat or car?
_____ The highest academic degree?
_____ The brightest, best-behaved children?
_____ The best-looking spouse?

Have you successfully said good-bye to using these people, places, and things as false gods?

_____ "We commit to making God the third leg of our marriage."
_____ "We commit to forgiveness."

Don't forget the occasional need to "forgive" God—and to come into a closer relationship with Him.

Encompass More of God

One of the women sitting around that conference table in the Minirth-Meier Clinic with Dr. Hemfelt's group was Linda. She did what all those old romance novels and feel-good movies used to tout: She defied her father's wishes to marry the man she loved. Daddy was wealthy. He could not abide a young man who left law school and essentially dropped out of polite society in order to pursue an art career. Despite that, Linda's husband carved a successful niche for himself in art circles, relations between Linda and her daddy remained cold and restrained from the engagement right up to his death.

With his passing, during Linda's Third Passage of marriage, she found herself in a profound spiritual crisis. The God of her prior Christian convictions appeared to be far too unfair and vengeful to warrant worship. She dwelt to the point of obsession on the tragedies that struck believers and unbelievers. She could not be reconciled to them. Because her crisis of faith coincided closely with her father's death, her pastoral counselor sent her to us.

To make a long therapy story short, Linda figured out that the death of her father had triggered within her the memories of all that pain she felt when her human father rejected her. She had projected the pain and injustice together upon her heavenly Father. Only after she grieved all that pain out, and released it, could she come back and embrace her heavenly Father. And embrace Him she did, more profoundly than she had ever known Him before.

Unresolved issues can and do spill over into the Third Passage, or wherever they are triggered by some event. And they can bar union with God just as easily as they bar intimacy with your spouse. If you have trouble reaching new depths of one-ness and understanding with God, look to your past for clues. Is something back there damaging your faith now?

Karl Jung believes you do not come to a true mature spiritual acceptance of God until the second half of life. Only now, in this Third Passage, can you get down to the deepest levels of spiritual insight. There are two archaic and distorted views of God you may have to dismiss first. One is the Santa Claus God, who can supply the grocery list of needs you present Him in prayer. The second is the harsh and vengeful Scorekeeper God who's planning to punish you for all your wrongs. Both are supported by selected Scripture verses. Neither represents the true God when all Scripture is viewed.

How much of your past is coloring your view of God now? First, what are your human father's (or adoptive father's) characteristics? *(Loving and supportive, for instance, or demanding and harsh?)*

1. _____
2. _____
3. _____

What are your mother's characteristics? *(Forgiving and understanding of your problems, for instance, or distant and uninterested in your activities?)*

1. _____
2. _____
3. _____

Now what are God's characteristics as you see them? *(Do you see Him as remote and detached, or as a Father who supports you when you're feeling lost or depressed?)*

1. _____
2. _____
3. _____

Compare the lists. Your parents may indeed reflect the Heavenly Father—and some do, because that's what parents are supposed to do according to the divine plan—or you may be projecting your earthly parents' image upon the heavenly one. Are you coloring your view of God in a limited way by your memories of your parents? Give the point as much thought as possible. Lord willing, it will lead to deeper insight.

Mid-Level Items

"Those are the big, over-riding concepts to consider." Dr. Hemfelt told the group. "Now let's look at the mid-level contract items—the ones that help you negotiate the terms of the contract.

"Remember the specifics in that inventory of dreams and realities we did earlier?" Dr. Hemfelt asked.

"Which dreams were those?" Rick asked.

"The ones you listed in the exercise where you first stated your dreams and then followed up with the reality of the situation. They were on such subjects as your mate, job, children, and social life." Dr. Hemfelt answered.

"Oh yeah. I saw how many of my dreams weren't coming true," Rick said.

"That will help you for this next step." Dr. Hemfelt said. "Now I want each of you to think of those dreams still within your reach. What if you modified them some? Made them more attainable. You're much too young to abandon all your dreams now. Perhaps by restructuring them somewhat, you can still have a shot at those dreams. What can you improve? Sex? Financial status? How can you go about it? Write that into the contract."

"How do we do that?" Nancy asked.

"Just as we explored the basis of any committing statements earlier, use the same technique for crystallizing your dreams in the contract. For example. . ." Dr. Hemfelt said. He went on to read down another list of statements like the ones below.

We invite you to also discuss the following items with your

spouse. Now is the time to help each other realize your most precious dreams. There is still ample time left in your lives together to do this.

How About You?

_____ "We can still realize these hopes and dreams (for example, 'Maybe we could still own our own business on a very small scale' "):

_____

_____

_____

"These are some practical ways to reach those goals (for example, *If we start our own business on a small scale, I could continue my full-time job to give us security in the transition*' "):

_____

_____

_____

A friend of ours once related the following story. He was a pastor in a rural community; his wife an artist. Late in their Third Passage of marriage they stumbled upon a realized dream. Their two boys had already been through college and were on their own. Both of them had been dabbling in various hobbies for years. His wife discovered a knack for writing through some articles she had done for the local newspaper. Her dream became to write a novel. Whether it was a success or not wasn't the point, she wanted to write one. He applauded it.

He summarized his feelings to us one day: "I feel that I should support Mary as her mate and best friend. I want to help her reach her full potential in life by encouraging her all along the way in whatever dream she's chasing."

During the latter part of this Third Passage, many couples have increasing free time to pursue some of their dreams. The best stance is to encourage each other during this pursuit.

Not all dreams will be realized. Which is why we suggest you carefully examine your list of dreams and adjust them—weed out the ones you don't really want and rework the ones you do into more attainable standards. Then go after the ones you want and let go of the ones you don't or won't reach.

Some dreams will never be achieved. Things will go wrong. Here is the place to make the commitment to the grief process. "Commit to grief? How dismal!" you protest. "Not at all!" we assure you. Healthy grieving will bring peace and ease the pain of disappointment and frustration. Grieving brings you to terms with reality. It is the only way to expunge anger and prevent the inward-turning of anger into depression.

_____ "We commit to grieving all losses."

Writing the Contract

At the next group session, Dr. Hemfelt discussed the nitty-gritty of writing the contract with the participants. We invite you and your spouse to do the same.

Page 184 shows an example of what your renewed contract can look like. Adjust this basic outline to fit your unique situation. Maybe you'd like to add Parenting as an item in the contract if that is an issue in your current relationship.

For the first item, remember when you analyzed your mate's positive and negative attributes in Chapter 3? Use that analysis in a mutual promise to work at minimizing the negatives (or irritations) and to affirm and praise the positives *on a regular, frequent basis.* Be specific about needs and preferences in this part.

_____ "I commit to affirmation of positive factors in my spouse."
_____ "I commit to attention and care toward minimizing the negatives I contribute."

Then state at least one positive attribute that you admire and appreciate in each other. Even more important than putting them in writing, make a commitment to verbally recognize these positive traits in each other on a regular (daily would be best) basis.

Next, go back to the statements you discussed under commitments to each other, marriage and God. Focus them for the contract, covering the items we mention in numbers 2 through 4 in our example of the renewed contract.

The Renewed Marriage Contract

1. Statement of affirmation; at least one attribute each person admires and appreciates in the other

2. Statement of extent of commitment to the marriage

3. Promise of fidelity

4. Statement of faith, embracing:
   a. Each person's individual statement of faith
   b. Clearly stated common ground
   c. Statement of tolerance (and limits of tolerance)

5. Statement of recognition of old, dysfunctional hidden agendas

6. Declaration of new agendas to redress dysfunctions

7. Sexual contract, including:
   a. Recognition of difficulties or shortcomings in present sexual relations
   b. Steps to improve relations and/or explore new techniques
   c. Details of frequency if frequency is an issue

8. Review of items in old contract, with updates and revisions as necessary

9. Details of everyday life (request for romantic nights out) established through give-and-take (be specific)

10. Agreement to periodically review and update (anniversaries are a good time)

For items 5 and 6, discuss together any areas that need adjustment in your current relationship. How about any tasks not successfully completed from the Third Passage? Look back to the quiz you both took in Chapter 9. Were there any areas that needed improving? Be honest. Everyone should have at least something to put down here. Maybe it has to do with your personal identity and marriage identity. Look over the following questions and answer them together:

- In Passage Three, I am aware of the following hidden agendas that have been distracting our marriage. (For example, "In recent years I have felt the power struggle between us more acutely. Although I hate to admit it, I know I constantly try to one-up you in controlling our finances.")

  1. _____
  2. _____
  3. _____
  4. _____
  5. _____

- As a part of statement 5 of our renewed marriage contract, recognize that these hidden agendas have more to do with the family I grew up in than they have to do with you. I acknowledge this recognition in the following ways (for example, "I know I am extremely sensitive to control issues in Passage Three because I saw my father totally dominate my mother in the mid-life years"):

  1. _____
  2. _____
  3. _____
  4. _____
  5. _____

- As an aspect of statement 6 in our renewed contract, I pledge myself to pursue the following new agendas to balance our marriage and enhance our shared identity (for example, "I know I have demanded far too much control in our finances. I pledge to approach all major financial decisions as a mutual decision. I pledge to try to hear fairly your input on our financial direction"):

  1. _____
  2. _____

3. _____

4. _____

5. _____

Rick and Nancy found that their personal identities were well established. They listed the marriage identity as an item needing work and effort in the years ahead. Through their counseling, they were able to see that deep down, they both wanted the marriage to continue.

An area of new agendas needing work may also be parenting. Look over the following questions. Answer them together as a couple to see if you have successfully negotiated the parenting aspects of this passage.

- What is the best aspect of our parenting style?

  _____
  _____
  _____

- What area of our parenting needs most improvement?

  _____
  _____
  _____

- In my opinion, what am I doing right as a father/mother?

  _____
  _____
  _____

- In my opinion, what do I need to improve on as a father/mother?

  _____
  _____
  _____

- How are our children doing as they approach, or are in the midst of, adolescence?

  _____
  _____
  _____

- What are some changes we need to make to accommodate their growth into young adults?

  _____

_____

_____

• What are the rules we expect our children to abide by?

_____

_____

_____

• What are the consequences we will enforce for them when they stray from these rules?

_____

_____

_____

Consequences must be enforceable and they must relate to the transgression done. For example, if a teenager is out past curfew with the family car, an appropriate consequence would be invoking the privilege of driving the car.

• What books can we read to encourage us as parents? (There are far too many excellent titles on the market to recommend here. Ask your pastor or close friends for suggestions.)

_____

_____

_____

If you find an area involving parenting that needs assistance (and frankly we'd be surprised if you haven't—the teen years are by far the most challenging) put the issues down as part of number 6 of the contract.

Number 7 is self-explanatory. Recommit to your sexual relationship in writing. Put down any areas where you want to make adjustments. Use the negotiating process, discuss any give and take. Perhaps the woman says, "I want more cuddling and romance." Perhaps the man says, "I want more frequency." Be specific on what your needs are. You can even try an arrangement for a while. If it doesn't work, go back and renegotiate; change the contract to make your sexual relationship satisfying to both of you. The object is not an iron-clad contract, but the process of making one. Use it as a dynamic process.

For number 8, if you prepared a contract as part of your First or Second Passage of marriage, now is the time to look it over. Discard any items that no longer apply and carry over items that are still valid today. (For example, a couple may discover that the time pledged to establishing a career in Passages One and Two cannot be scaled back in Passage Three.)

Number 9 is hard work and fun. Under this statement, a couples needs to plan how the daily business of life will be carried out in Passage Three—who carries out the trash; who cooks the meals; who pays the bills; who waits up late for the teenagers coming home from their dates.

The fun comes when you recommit to dating each other. Remember when you were sixteen—how you took extra care in planning or anticipating that big date? Although it's healthy to grieve lost youth now, it's not healthy to lose the romance of your youth. You may have grown up in a time when the guy did all the romancing and pursuing. Now, in your marriage, it's healthy for the gal to participate just as fully.

Get your calendars out and plan dates on a regular basis. You can schedule the dates around special events such as concerts, lectures or when you have free time (a weekend even—when you were a teenager you didn't get to date for a whole weekend. Now you can).

Each of you should arrange at least one date a month around an event or activity that will please your mate. Make sure the environment breeds romance. It will help if you follow these simple rules:

1. The couple should be *alone* together. This is not the time for socializing with other couples or families.
2. The couple *cannot* discuss problems or troublesome issues in their family or business lives. (There are other more appropriate times for this other type of sharing.)
3. The couple should plan to do something special—out-of-the-ordinary.
4. If you are planning the date, plan something you think you both would like to do.

The final item of the contract (number 10) commits you both to frequently look over and update the contract. As we mentioned before, use this process as a dynamic one. Periodically reviewing and updating contract items will keep your marriage vibrant, growing, and exciting.

Mend What Needs Mending

After completing your renewed contract, now is also the time to look the inevitable losses of your life straight in the face. You must confront them and resolve them now before it's too late. As we age, so do those around us. If we haven't mended our relationships with those around us, we may never get another chance. Do it now before it's too late. Answer the following questions. They will help you see your areas that need mending.

1. Who are the people who will be most missed in your life?
   _____
   _____
   _____

2. Is there anyone you need to mend a relationship with or tell them something you haven't yet?
   _____
   _____
   _____

3. When I hear the statements: "Mend what needs mending. Say what needs saying." I think of the following:
   _____
   _____
   _____

4. The inevitable losses I know are coming are:
   _____
   _____
   _____

5. The inevitable losses that have already hit me are:
   _____
   _____
   _____

Now that you've said good-bye, it's time to say hello.

Hello to the Future

Nancy and Rick's marriage was back on the road to fulfillment and enrichment with a brand new contract at work. They looked forward to the rest of their Third Passage.

Some of the couples in Dr. Hemfelt's group, however, were entering the Fourth Passage of marriage. For them, this new contract represented approximately twenty-five years of their lives. At the end of this Third Passage, they had spent more time with each other than with their parents.

Your history together may be as long. It will be part of the blessing you will take into the Renewing Love passage of marriage—the Fourth. To fully appreciate these blessings, you may want to read our next book, *Renewing Love*, the fourth in our series on the Passages of Marriage.

If you, as other couples in Dr. Hemfelt's group, have successfully navigated the various passages of marriage to this point, you can look forward to the joys and challenges offered you in the passages to come. Look back at page 21 in Chapter 1 for a list of the passages of marriage and associated tasks. Think of it as a navigational chart. Celebrate those ports (passages) visited and conquered. Plot a course for the ones to come. The winds are good and your sails are full. You are headed into the sunset and it's gorgeous!

Appendix

Summary Questions Reflecting This Third Passage

Consider these questions at your leisure. Think about them. Many cannot be answered with a simple yes or no. They are thought-provokers. Let them be a reference point and a guide as you trace your way through the Third Passage.

1. Am I free to be honest and open about my feelings?

2. Do I feel I must win when we disagree?

3. Do I allow my spouse to dictate my mood by his/hers?

4. Do I participate with genuine interest in our sex life?

5. Do I seek to control my spouse by any chronic negative behavior?

6. Can I honestly say I have a life separate from my marriage as well as within it?

7. Am I confident of my spouse's sincerity regarding our marital vows?

8. Am I able to separate and identify my thoughts and feelings from my spouse's?

9. Am I confident that my life goes on with or without my spouse?

10. Are the moments of lovey-dovey closeness and howling fights less polarized now than in prior years?

11. Has the newness of my spouse's imperfections worn off and acceptance set in?

12. Are discreet issues (such as parenting, for example) recognized as only part of the marriage rather than being allowed to dominate the whole picture?

13. Overall, do I feel more at peace with my relationship now than in earlier years?

14. Am I careful not to pull outsiders into our conflicts?

15. Am I harboring a list of major resentments about previous conflicts?

16. Do I do unto my spouse what my spouse has done to me, or do I seek to do unto him/her what I want done to me? (Am I succumbing to the temptation to "dish it right back out when the situation arises"?)

17. Am I able to move on when conflict arises and avoid blaming my spouse and others?

18. Am I free of any desire for an extramarital affair?

19. Am I still willingly committed for a lifetime?

20. Am I making the effort to move in the same direction as my spouse?

21. Am I in agreement with my spouse as to priorities in life regarding family and work? Partial agreement?

22. Am I left with a sense of balance in life; comfort that is not simply complacency?